Running with Champions

A MIDLIFE JOURNEY ON THE IDITAROD TRAIL

Lisa Frederic

Alaska Northwest Books®

I would especially like to thank my dear champions:
Tahoe, Lassen, Salem, Houston, Marco, Alto, Utah, Hardtack,
Bismarck, Latte, Ice, Shuman, Potter, Coco, Shasta, Portland, and Reno.

Thank you, David, for tending the home fires; Donna and Jeff King, for taking
me in; Tricia Brown, Sherry Simpson, Kurt Hellweg, Dan Kosla, Martha Bristow, Ronald Spatz,
and Leslie Fields, for their kind encouragement and editing;
and my dear neighbors in Village Islands for keeping the skiffs bailed
and the bears away from the house while I've been away.

Text © 2006 by Lisa Frederic
All photographs © Lisa Frederic unless otherwise indicated.

Chapter 9, "300 Miles—in a Day or Two," is excerpted from litsite.alaska.edu.

Library of Congress Cataloging-in-Publication Data
Frederic, Lisa, 1959-
Running with champions : a midlife journey on the Iditarod Trail / by Lisa Frederic.
    p. cm.
ISBN-13: 978-0-88240-616-9 (softbound) 1. Frederic, Lisa, 1959- 2. Iditarod (Race)
3. Women mushers—Alaska—Kodiak—Biography. 4. Mushers—Alaska—Kodiak—
Biography. 5. Sled dog racing—Alaska. I. Title.
SF440.15.F72 2006
798.8'309798—dc22   2006006128

The Iditarod Trail Sled Dog Race is a registered trademark of the Iditarod Trail Committee.

FRONT COVER PHOTO: Tom Walker.
BACK COVER PHOTO: Curt Door, Cabela's   BACK COVER INSET PHOTO: Jeff and Donna King

Alaska Northwest Books®
An imprint of Graphic Arts Books
P.O. Box 56118
Portland, OR 97238-6118
(503) 254-5591

EDITOR: Tricia Brown
COVER DESIGN: Elizabeth Watson
INTERIOR DESIGN: Constance Bollen, CB Graphics
CARTOGRAPHY: Gray Mouse Graphics

PRAISE FOR *RUNNING WITH CHAMPIONS*

"This is an inspiring story of a middle-aged woman who sets out to live her dream—pushing herself beyond her own physical and emotional limits—to achieve something she never thought possible. A great journey to follow."
—Gary Paulsen

"If you wanted to run the 1,200 mile Iditarod with a crazed 850-pound team of sixteen huskies—then read Lisa Frederic's superb account of misadventures and success. She's forty, slightly built, a rookie completely new to the sport, but full of resolve. After a winter's apprentice with Iditarod Champ Jeff King, she runs the Iditarod—and reminds me that great adventures are more than just good planning."
—Joe Runyan, 1989 Iditarod Champion

"I thoroughly enjoyed this vivid account of a spirited individual with a zest for life who managed to go from curious observer of the Iditarod to crossing under the burled arch in Nome herself in just a few short years. I have a hunch some unsuspecting reader of this book will one day make such a life journey of his or her own."
—Stan Hooley, Executive Director,
Iditarod Trail Committee

"For Lisa, the dogs were champions long before they won a race. Their journey, hers and the dogs, needed no trophy to celebrate success. This is a great story for anyone who dreams of 'doing it'—no matter what 'It' is. If I had a tail, I'd be wagging it!"
—Jeff King, winner of his fourth Iditarod, with Salem winning the coveted Golden Harness Award, 2006

Contents

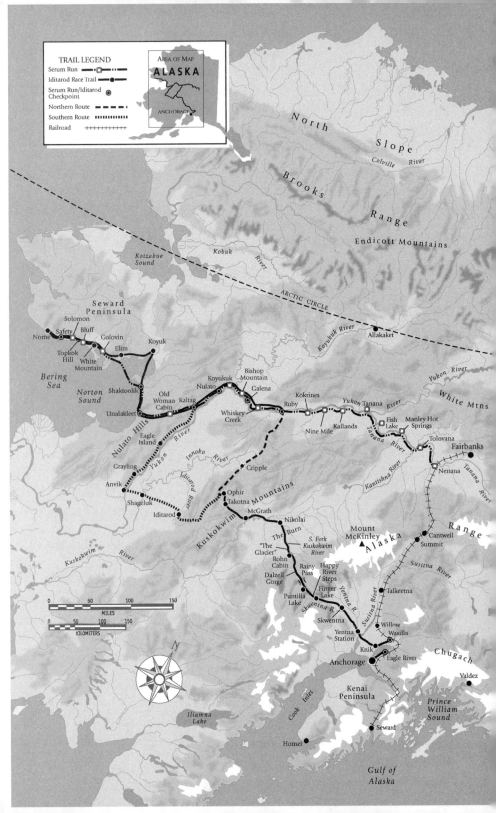

TRAIL LEGEND
Serum Run
Iditarod Race Trail
Serum Run/Iditarod
Checkpoint
Northern Route
Southern Route
Railroad

AREA OF MAP
ALASKA

ANCHORAGE

North
Slope

Colville River

Brooks

Range

Endicott Mountains

Kotzebue Sound

Kobuk River

ARCTIC CIRCLE

Koyukuk River

Allakaket

Seward Peninsula

Solomon
Nome
Safety
Bluff
Topkok Hill
White Mountain
Golovin
Elim
Koyuk

Bering Sea

Norton Sound

Shaktoolik

Unalakleet

Old Woman Cabin

Kaltag

Koyukuk

Nulato

Bishop Mountain

Galena

Koyukuk River

Kokrines

Ruby

Yukon River

Tanana

Tanana River

White Mtns

Whiskey Creek

Nine Mile

Kallands

Fish Lake

Manley Hot Springs

Tolovana

Fairbanks

Nenana

Nulato Hills

Eagle Island

Yukon River

Innoko River

Grayling

Anvik

Shageluk

Iditarod

Cripple

Iditarod River

Ophir

Takotna

McGrath

Nikolai

The Burn

S. Fork Kuskokwim River

Mount McKinley

Alaska

Range

Cantwell

Summit

Kantishna River

Tanana River

Kuskokwim Mountains

Kuskokwim River

"The Glacier"
Rohn Cabin
Dalzell Gorge

Rainy Pass

Happy River Steps

Finger Lake

Puntilla Lake

Skwentna R.

Yentna R.

Susitna River

Talkeetna

Willow
Wasilla

Yentna Station

Knik

Anchorage

Eagle River

Chugach

Valdez

Kenai Peninsula

Cook Inlet

Iliamna Lake

Seward

Prince William Sound

Homer

Gulf of Alaska

0   50   100   150
MILES

0   50   100   150
KILOMETERS

N

Introduction

※

Learning Curves and a Long, Long Trail

The dogs were screaming to go; the leaders slamming into their harnesses, trying to free the sled from its earthly tethers. As we moved forward, volunteers gripped the towline, digging their heels into the snowy street in an attempt to control the team. As usual, the starting chute ran right down the middle of downtown Anchorage's Fourth Avenue, but it was still a surprise to see high-rises so close to my dog team.

Though many of the teams had already left, many more were still waiting their turn. The din of hundreds of barking dogs, echoing off the buildings, made a tremendous pitch that matched my nerves. My husband, David, joined me on the sled runners, but even his extra weight did little to faze the team. The dogs strained against their lines like leashed wildcats.

People bundled in their heaviest winter coats crowded the streets, their outfits softly filling any vacant spaces between them. They called out greetings, their mittens padding a muffled applause as each team, dragging a group of faithful volunteers, went rushing by. Like a rubber band pulled tighter and tighter, the tension amplified with each step closer to the starting line; photographers positioned for close-ups, and complete strangers adamantly waved. I could hear my name bandied about by the announcers: "commercial fisher from Kodiak . . . wild Alaskan salmon . . . training dogs for three-time Iditarod champion Jeff King . . . "

This can't really be happening. Just five years ago, I knew nothing about this crazy world of dog mushing. It had all begun with a vacation that had gone awry. Going to Nome as a tourist had turned my life upside down. I looked down at the sled as if for the first time and felt vaguely puzzled seeing that the mittened hands gripping the handle bow were my own. *What in the hell had I signed up for?*

Denny, a veterinarian I knew from volunteer work with the Iditarod, leaned her face close to mine. Ignoring the bedlam that surrounded us, she calmly smiled and tucked in some hair that had escaped my fur hat.

"It's going to be fine. You're going to do great," she said, and it was almost a whisper, but I heard her. The overhead speakers then exploded with numbers reverberating off the tall buildings. Suddenly I fully understood their significance.

"Five . . . four . . . three . . . two . . . ONE! She's OFF! Lisa Frederic, the rookie from Kodiak, Alaska, is on her way to Nome!"

CHAPTER 1

Not Exactly Bluegrass Country

*M*y free fall into the world of sled dogs came quickly, and late in life. I had lived in Alaska for a long time, but had paid little attention to the Iditarod Trail Sled Dog Race. I had read about the pioneers and the gold rushes, but in my twenties and thirties I was busy building a house and career on the island of Kodiak. Snow was not something I could count on; sled dogs were not a hot topic of conversation in my life on fishing boats.

I had come to Alaska looking for a summer job when I was twenty-one years old. There were plenty of other kids doing the same thing, working in canneries processing salmon and then king crab, most earning money for college or plane tickets to exotic countries. We lived in tents—illegally—at the edge of town. It rained almost constantly, not gently or softly, but in a roar and with great force.

The Kodiak Archipelago lies one hundred and fifty miles southwest of Anchorage, a cluster of craggy slate islands shaped by the violent storms of the Gulf of Alaska. Food was ridiculously expensive and every building in the town of Kodiak seemed to need a new coat of paint. Yet I loved the mountains rising sharply up from the sea, loved the long, black beaches edged by an ocean so cold and blue my eyes watered and my lungs hurt just looking at it. I loved the feeling of being on the edge of somewhere.

With the first stinging sleet, the summer crews fled and I meekly called my family in Kentucky to say I was staying. I had no clear plan, but had no desire to leave. By spring I had started fishing commercially, working on small boats and ignoring the pleas of my parents to "come home and finish college." But the harbor was alive with people my age earning good money doing hard work. There was an addicting "sense of community" between the fishers and the environment that surrounded them.

I had come to Alaska with the usual dreams of log cabins and a winter wonderland, yet ended up living in a place I could rarely ski. When Libby Riddles and Susan Butcher were dominating the Iditarod in the eighties I was impressed, and yet I was already working in "a man's world," so the gender issue was only vaguely interesting. It was obvious that Alaska was the place a person could strive to do what they wished—whatever their sex. It was just one of many reasons I had stayed.

I met David, who at twenty-nine had decided to escape a career as a research psychologist. For several years we bankrolled our travels around the world by gill-netting salmon in a remote bay on the west side of the island. While picking sockeye out of the nets, we dreamed up exciting itineraries: Belize, Nepal, Thailand, Antarctica.

It wasn't until 1997 that Nome landed on our destination list, and we decided to see the finish of the Iditarod. It seemed like a classy Alaskan thing to do, and we had extra airline miles. We made reservations to include David's mom, Dena, and a neighbor from Kodiak.

Being an Alaskan, I knew the Iditarod began each year on the first weekend of March in Anchorage, the state's largest city. Once the mushers left the urban comforts behind, though, they entered a wilderness journey that covered more than a thousand miles, and since no highways followed the trail, there was no way to drive to any of the twenty checkpoints where the mushers resupplied. The route passed through a handful of villages—most quite tiny, with just a couple hundred residents.

Though the race generally took ten days, weather conditions—good or bad—could have a huge effect on when the first-place winner got to Nome. Such was the case with our trip. Our timing was off, and we arrived the morning after champion Martin Buser crossed the finish line.

Figuring that our vacation was ruined, I called the Chamber of Commerce. The woman laughed, "Oh, don't worry—you'll find plenty to do."

Pictures of Nome during the gold-rush era showed hundreds of white tents in rows parallel to the sea. Nearly a century later, there still seemed to be a fascinating lack of building codes. It was common to see a lovely, old-style Victorian wooden house on one lot, with a plywood shanty just twenty feet away on the next piece of property. Next to that may be a cedar home or a packing crate that housed sled dogs. I couldn't tell what the status symbols were—a new truck parked out front, an antique dogsled on top of the roof, or a collection of fuel drums in the yard.

Nearly blocking off the center of the main street, a huge burled log formed an arch over the finish line. Burned into the wood were the words "End of Iditarod Sled Dog Race." My eyes watered from the cold as I peered up at this Alaska icon, and my feet were quickly turning into frozen blocks. My nose wouldn't stop running. Considering I was on vacation, I was pretty miserable.

A siren went off, and soon I could see a dog team skirting the traffic down the street. At first the dogs seemed frightened by the crowd, but then at the sound of a woman's voice, they pricked their ears forward and seemed to lighten their step. People called out encouragement as they traveled the last block, and I saw wagging tails as they reached the finish line.

The musher stopped the sled under the arch, barely glancing up at the symbol that marked the end of his journey. He seemed huge in his snowsuit, like an astronaut. He shyly glanced at the crowd and awkwardly hugged his family, then brushed past the officials, shuffling along the length of the team. He ran his hand down the body of each animal, wrapping his giant arms briefly around several. When he reached the front, he sank to his knees next to the two leaders and buried his face in their coats. For a second I stared, but then had to turn my head. Though surrounded by so many people, the moment seemed so personal, so private. ✓

When he stood up, his eyes were bright and wet. The crowds seemed to confuse him, but the emotion on his face confused me. He seemed <u>more grateful than victorious, more humbled than triumphant.</u> As the crowd of well-wishers closed in around him, he kept breaking away to caress a dog. Several times he seemed to pause, anxiously looking back to his team.

I noticed that they, too, though surrounded by people lavishing praise and caresses, frequently searched him out of the crowd. When their eyes met, they locked for an instant—as if they were back alone on the trail.

When the woman joined the musher on the sled runners, several dogs turned and wagged their tails. For a moment the couple held each other tightly, then he leaned back to stare silently into her face. She smoothed back the frosted edge to his fur ruff and touched his cheek, smiling. His eyes spoke clearly.

I have so much to tell!

I was surprised at the rush of emotion I felt. I was not expecting this. I was merely a tourist. I was just in Nome to see the sights and watch the end of a dog race. This was just one of many things highlighted on the travel brochure. Why did I feel such a wrenching sense of wonder at the scene in front of me?

For the rest of the day I seemed to walk in a private bubble. The city sounded the fire alarm whenever a team approached, giving everyone a few minutes to get dressed in their heavy parkas and make it down to the finish line. Even as we were taking in the sights around town, I found myself straining to hear the siren, ready to throw on my coat and see the next team, to watch the mushers and their families, to study the volunteers working on the race.

Over the next few days I found myself staring at the mushers who had finished the Iditarod. They seemed so different from their portraits in the official program I had bought before the race. Their cheeks were burned with frostbite and their lips were swollen. Many walked stiffly. But I couldn't look away. Something in their eyes mesmerized me.

By the end of the week, we found ourselves jammed into a local hall for the Iditarod's traditional Awards Banquet. I listened as the mushers retold their trail stories, often long, drawn-out affairs, but I drank in every word. Finally, I leaned over and whispered in my mother-in-law's ear, "I want to find a way to become a volunteer for this Iditarod." I was pushing forty and yet there was envy in her voice.

"If I were your age, I would certainly do it," she said nodding.

Later that night, I watched the lights of the city disappear as the jet took off from Nome. The night sky was sharp—so crystalline I could see everything as we crossed the state: whole mountain ranges passing silently below, silky white threads of rivers winding through the frozen tundra, valleys cutting sharply into mysterious depths. I couldn't quite make it out, but I knew the Iditarod Trail was somewhere down there and I strained to see indentations in the vast whiteness.

Hale Bopp was so close it felt like a private showing. When the jet changed directions, the Big Dipper came into full view through my window, and I had to lean my head against the pane. I hadn't slept well for days. This event, this thing called the Iditarod Trail Sled Dog Race, seemed to have so many facets, so many things I loved—history, wilderness, a family of volunteers, remote Alaskan communities, and of course, dogs.

Alaska was in my soul. I had known it for twenty years; yet what I had seen during the past week had made me simply dizzy with possibilities. I wanted to find out more.

CHAPTER 2

A Volunteer on the Iditarod Trail

*I*n the mid-eighties, after several years crewing for other people, David and I had bought our own fishing operation. Eventually we had found property fifty miles from the closest road and began the tedious job of building a home in a remote cove of Uganik Bay. I had always imagined living on a farm in the country, not in a wilderness refuge on a remote island. It was a far cry from my southern heritage; my parents had always thought I would be a dental assistant in the Bluegrass State.

For nearly two decades I had craved the adrenaline rush that came in the pursuit of wild salmon on the open ocean. I had loved working fast and furiously when the fish were hitting; the days turning into weeks until fatigue was so deep that the most basic elements of life—food and sleep—had became exotic fantasies. We were never going to get rich, but we made a good living with a great product.

The home we had built was perched on the edge of the sea, and every single board was hauled up the cliff with ropes and pulleys. We had no telephone and made our own electricity with old solar panels. In the winter the weather was often so bad that no seaplanes could land in the bay, and thus no mail was delivered. Communication with anyone outside our community of twelve was cut off so often, the neighbors had become like family. We had our differences, but we unconditionally accepted them. The views out our windows were indeed the envy of every visitor to the bay, and yet no one really understood the price we paid.

It had been a good way to live, one that I loved, though the physical work had aged my body beyond its years. On a good day's fishing I often did several thousand deep-knee bends transferring fish from boat to boat. My back felt the abuse of rolling logs on frozen beaches in the winters, hauling them in and out of the skiff, then up a cliff where I split the sections into pieces that would fit into the woodstove. A couple of fingers were permanently swollen and didn't open all the way, an elbow painfully creaked and my back periodically froze up—but generally the dues seemed a small price. Living and loving the island of Kodiak was like being addicted to a bipolar lover.

But in the months that followed the trip to Nome, I thought of little else. I read everything I could about the Iditarod and talked to friends who worked on the race. By fall I had secured a volunteer position on the trail for the next March. I began collecting arctic gear from secondhand stores until I had a bulky pile of clothing. Leaking goose-down feathers and patched with duct tape, the gear left me doubtful about my mobility once I was fully dressed. I was warned to pack as lightly as possible since the volunteers were flown to the checkpoints in small planes, but my parka alone weighed nearly thirty pounds!

Small planes on skis flew the volunteers and supplies to the various supply spots along the trail. Some were villages; some were tents set up along a frozen river. I was assigned to Rohn, which was a remote cabin somewhere between Rainy Pass and an area everyone called "The Burn." A small log cabin replaced the original roadhouse that had served the Iditarod Trail in the early part of the century, and now it served as the checkpoint.

Before the era of roads, a complex trail system wove through the territory of Alaska, leading to the various regions where gold was being discovered. In 1898 the Klondike attracted thousands of people north, but when gold discoveries started waning there, other locations became the meccas of the north—Ophir, Nome, Fairbanks, Kantishna—countless regions where towns sprung up overnight. Since most travel was by dog team, shelters or roadhouses were built about a day's journey apart on most of these trails. The roadhouse at Rohn had been on the main trail to the mining district of Iditarod, which lay several hundred miles farther to the west. It would have been a welcome sight to the gold stampeders, a sign that they had made it through the Alaska Range, some of the highest mountains in the land.

In the early twentieth century, dog teams were an essential component of life in the Interior and coastal areas of Alaska. Nome had the famed "Alaska Sweepstakes" that pitted competitive breeders and their dogs against each other. Many of these same animals were essential members of dog teams that carried a life-saving serum from Nenana to Nome in 1925. In temperatures that often reached –50° to –60°F, twenty mushers, including the famous Leonhard Seppala, relayed a diphtheria serum across Alaska in an astonishing five days. Dogs like Balto, Togo, Gold Fang, and many others were the superheroes of the day, their fame bringing them international attention. Several even spent the rest of their lives on lecture tours that were popular at the time.

But by the early 1960s, the introduction of snowmobiles—or "snow machines" as they're called in Alaska—had nearly replaced the population of sled dogs in the state. A handful of people had recreational teams, and a few sprint races were still held annually, but generally sled dogs were losing their place in Alaska society. They were slipping into antiquity.

In the late 1960s, Dorothy Page, with the help of Joe Redington Sr. and other sled-dog enthusiasts, came up with the concept of a long-distance race over the old Iditarod Trail. In 1973, the first Iditarod was completed—having taken three weeks for the winner and nearly a month for the final musher to cross the finish line. The huge success of the event had turned around the demise of sled-dog racing in North America. The sport had regained its position not only in Alaska, but also in northern communities all over the world.

Dorothy Page passed away in 1989, and Joe Redington Sr. carried on the often-thankless job of promoting and organizing a race across a winter wilderness. Though many had been involved and had contributed in countless ways, the success of the race was generally attributed to one man, and Redington had earned the title, "Father of the Iditarod."

I had been privileged to see Joe mush across the finish line on my very first day as a tourist in Nome. He had come into town in thirty-sixth place—at eighty years old. His wife, Vi, had greeted him under the burled arch, delightfully regal in a purple satin hat that would have made Princess Diana envious. Though totally out of place here in the Arctic, it somehow fit the scene perfectly. This couple was indeed Alaska's royalty.

Now, as a volunteer at Rohn, I was joining thousands of others who had helped keep the race going since its founding. Several feet of snow capped the cabin's roof, moose antlers hung above the handmade door, and an intoxicating smell of wood smoke and spruce trees perfumed the air. When I saw it, I had to smile. I had left Kentucky twenty years earlier in search of this exact setting.

The "Iditarod Air Force"—a squadron of private planes flown by volunteers—brought in more volunteers and a mountain of supplies that we carefully organized. I drilled the pilots about where they had come from, which checkpoint they would fly to next. They spoke of landing on frozen rivers and primitive airstrips; the names they casually mentioned seemed so strange to me: Ruby, Cripple, Ophir, the ghost town of Iditarod. These were the hot spots in the last great gold stampede that had drawn thousands of prospectors and entrepreneurs into this country. Sensing my excitement, they paused to describe the winding rivers, the valleys that held abandoned gold mines, the buffalo, and the herds of caribou.

My primary job would be parking teams and working with veterinarians who were taking care of "dropped" dogs. Dogs cannot be added during the race, but they can be left behind at the checkpoints, often as part of the musher's strategy. I was told it didn't really take sixteen dogs to pull a sled, and if one wasn't happy, or had even a minor injury, it was better just to send it home. The Iditarod Air Force flew the dogs out of the checkpoints to Anchorage, where they were reunited with their kennels.

Teams started arriving so fast that just as one was parked, another would arrive. Throughout that evening, the next day, and into the following night, I literally jogged between parking teams, pampering the dropped dogs and escorting teams back out onto the trail.

Most mushers stayed in Rohn just six hours, barely enough time to do their work and perhaps take a quick nap. Small fires flickered in the woods as they cooked hot meals for the dogs and repacked their sleds. Every single foot in the team was carefully examined and massaged with a creamy ointment. Bent over for hours in the cold, the mushers seemed to coo as they worked, the soft murmuring like the hymn of wood nymphs. I did the math, and my back began to ache just thinking about bending over long enough to massage sixty-four feet.

Only after the dogs were resting quietly did the mushers take a moment to care for their own needs. They crowded into the cabin, lining every spare inch of space with wet gloves, socks, and parkas. The aroma of wet dog and sweaty humans was nothing like the Kentucky stables I had worked in growing up. The woodstove turned the room into a funky-smelling sauna. However, this deep into the wilderness, there was an extravagance to being inside a warm building and no one complained about the details.

Throughout the night, I kept careful vigil over the dropped dogs. I mixed them hot soups of salmon, lamb, beef. I padded their beds with extra straw and was amazed at how gentle each one was. They were more like pets than working dogs. I fell in love with many: Arnold, who would not stop howling; Mercury, who wanted to play no matter what the hour; shy little Blackie, the sweetie owned by the grizzled old musher with a limp.

We had been working nonstop for nearly forty-two hours straight when we escorted the last two teams out of Rohn. I was tired and looked forward to taking off my boots, lying down anywhere flat, but knew sleep would not come easily. I was already planning on how to do it all over again.

For the next two years I lived for the next Iditarod. When I wasn't physically working for the race, I was counting the days until I was once again bundling into my parka, squeezing into some tiny plane on skis, and heading off to desolate villages in the Interior. I often found myself picking fish out of the net in the summer, reliving the events of the last Iditarod, staring at the photos, sniffing the air for snow.

Rick Swenson, a five-time Iditarod champion, summed up the feelings of mushers and volunteers alike: "In March, we do the Iditarod. This is just what we do." But for me, the other eleven months were becoming painfully long. A whole new planet seemed to be spinning just beyond this world of ocean and fish that I had settled into through the years on Kodiak. Something was stirring in my psyche that had lain dormant for nearly two decades. The sea now seemed almost flat, and I dreamed of the countless ways Eskimos described snow. I was consumed and going stir-crazy. I stared deeper into the photographs of people mushing, digging for hints into their mysterious world. Finally I came up with a vague plan.

David listened to my ideas and agreed I should do something. The books on the Iditarod that surrounded our bed were getting ridiculously deep, and though he had never read a single one, he could spout off a variety of names and facts just from listening to my babblings. He also knew my impatient nature.

It was a long shot, as I was older than most normal job applicants, but one night I finally wrote letters to several Iditarod mushers whom I admired. The addresses on the envelopes seemed so exotic—Manley Hot Springs, Big Lake, Denali Park; I felt like I was eighteen and applying for school abroad. For the next month, I anxiously waited for the mail plane to arrive and then plowed through the bills, catalogs, and letters with just one thing on my mind, as if I were waiting for a notice from Ed McMahon. I no longer walked, I skipped. I didn't hum, I sang.

CHAPTER 3

Good Coffee, but Short Coffee Breaks

Volunteering was great, but if I wanted to know more about sled dogs and the people who raised them, it meant finding a job as a dog handler. A dog handler is the person at the kennel whose primary job is caring for the dogs. Though most of them do run teams themselves, not everyone ends up competing in races. Obviously, the musher-owner cares for the dogs as well, but concentrates more on the training. The handler takes care of the more mundane tasks at the kennel—feeding, cleaning the dog yard, maintaining a variety of equipment—generally ensuring the kennel keeps operating smoothly.

David and I gingerly talked about the possibilities. For a while, life would change if I went away from our home in Uganik. Our house, like a farm, required constant work to keep it going. The power systems, the greenhouse, and the current building projects—something was always going on or going wrong, and if I left it would all be David's sole responsibility. Going away for a few weeks to volunteer for the Iditarod was one thing, but months apart was something more difficult. Who would lift the other end of long boards as the gear shed was being built? Who would light the candles at dinner?

He kept insisting that he wouldn't mind keeping things running smoothly. Living alone would be difficult, but he was a big boy. He had his own winter projects lined up—building a new shed, designing a boat, bookshelves for the library room. I felt guilty, almost ashamed, but we agreed I should go. All I could think about were sled dogs, and I needed to get it out of my system.

The musher letters I'd written proposed a "trial" period of employment; I couldn't commit myself to a full winter season. I was not a kid without other responsibilities. Since everything at home would be put on hold while I followed this whim, time was precious to me.

Jeff King was an Iditarod champion with a reputation of a fierce competitor. I had seen him at checkpoints and had been impressed with the focus he maintained, even when he was obviously exhausted. I had never seen a dog kennel before, but knew instinctively it was more work than glory. I wasn't afraid of hard work; I was looking for a professional environment. I wanted to learn the most about sled dogs as quickly as possible. At forty, I wanted a high learning curve. I wanted good coffee, but short coffee breaks.

I interviewed with the Kings and liked what I heard. They had three daughters and close to eighty dogs. Their "homestead" was in a small community south of the entrance of Denali Park. Surrounded by the snow country of Mount McKinley, it seemed like a perfect setting to learn about sled dogs. Donna was a well-known painter, and I was comforted to know that if the mushing thing didn't end up appealing, at least I would be near some good artwork. Having no clear idea what my life was going to be like, I agreed to move north to their place in January.

I rendezvoused with Jeff and his Danish handler, Morten, at a sled-dog race just outside of Anchorage. It was bittersweet saying good-bye to David. He was returning home to Uganik, while I was moving in with strangers. Periodically, over our last dinner together, I would have bouts of panic and get melancholy. *What in the hell was I doing? Who were these people I was going to live with? Why was I leaving my beautiful home on Kodiak Island?* When I got into the dog truck, I thought David was going to cry. As we pulled away, he looked so lonely standing next to our truck; I felt that familiar pang of guilt. *Was this fair?*

We pulled into the dog yard just after three in the morning. I was shown to my living quarters, a room above a storage shed that overlooked the kennel. The doghouses lay in neat, silhouetted patterns in the yard below me, and a steep ridge of white mountains rose high above the dark trees. I tried lying down for a while, but couldn't sleep. The northern lights were so bright; their shadows flickered on my pillow. I could watch them from the bed, but was too excited to lie still and moved to the window. To the north, the iridescent sheets of green and white lights shimmered across the sky, periodically tinted with rose hues. I thought of the night skies of Kodiak perpetually veiled in a gray mist.

It was still dark when my clock indicated it was morning. I carefully dressed in layer upon layer: a vest, wool sweaters, two pairs of long underwear. I kept peering out of the window, waiting for someone to start working in the yard. It was hours before anyone else got up, but by then I was soaked with sweat. I wondered if it was just the gear, or menopausal hot flashes.

I thought back to one of the telephone interviews when I had told Jeff, "You may need a little patience with me as I learn to dress for the severe cold." There had been such a long pause that for a moment, I thought the phone line had gone dead.

Finally, he replied slowly and evenly, "I'm not exactly known for my patience."

Wow, I had thought, there were no hidden clauses with this guy. When I relayed the story to David, nervously giggling, he shook his head. I wasn't exactly known for my patience either! I had a zero-tolerance policy with my salmon crews on several things, and any kind of tardiness had always driven me crazy. How would I handle being in the more vulnerable position of employee?

When I finally saw someone in the dog yard, I quickly bolted out the door. It was –22°F. I was sweating profusely and could hardly move in my outfit, but at least no one had waited for me.

Each dog had its own house with small openings to keep out the wind. These private homes were filled with straw to keep the dogs warm. The dogs were attached to long chains so they could run and touch noses with their neighbors. They all seemed pretty playful, racing around and wagging their tails. They barked, but never for very long, and I decided my mother-in-law's three dogs in California made much more noise than the whole dog yard full of Alaskan huskies.

Donna and Jeff's house sat on the edge of a frozen lake, surrounded by small ridges covered in spruce trees. The mountains then rose pretty quickly into a wall of peaks in all directions, but I was disappointed to hear we couldn't see Mount McKinley from the kennel. The community, known as Denali Park, was actually just a pocket of private land surrounded by Denali National Park. The mountain itself was a hundred miles away, beyond the ridges to the west.

After feeding the dogs and scooping the yard, Morten took a team out on a training run. When he came back, I helped unharness the dogs and return them to their houses. They seemed so happy, it was great fun. I cheerfully gathered up harnesses, hanging them on pegs according to size. Hurrying over to get the sled I sang out to Morten. "Where should I put this?"

He looked up at the sky. Thick clouds were beginning to crowd the mountain peaks to the north.

"It looks like it may snow—put it on the roof."

I carefully studied his expression. *Had I misunderstood?* I tilted my head in disbelief.

"On the *roof*?"

He nodded agreeably and continued working. His Scandinavian accent was quite strong, but he sounded serious. I was determined to do a good job and so only briefly hesitated. I started dragging the sled toward the barn. It had the only roof I could possibly imagine reaching. I had never lived where the snow got really deep. Obviously this must be why sleds were stored up high—like the caches I had seen in pictures.

I tried to appear casual. I knew the racing sleds were supposed to be especially light, but I still had my doubts. Could I lift the whole thing above my head? Since Morten wasn't offering to help, I reasoned the Dane was testing me. After commercial fishing for so long, I was used to cocky young men trying to challenge me. It may not be pretty, I decided, but I would certainly get the damn sled up on top of that roof.

To get close to the building, I had to climb onto a high pile of snow that was unfortunately very soft. Sinking down to my knees, I hauled the sled up alongside me. I briefly looked up at the roof, and then taking a deep breath, lifted the front of the sled toward the eaves. I hoped I could pivot it further skyward from there.

I heaved, missed, and it came back down next to me with a thud. Trying not to miss a beat, I immediately lifted again, but unfortunately, with each movement, I was sinking further in the snow. The roof was getting higher and farther away. I could feel Morten's eyes on me, but now when I used all my strength, the sled did not come anywhere near the roofline. Finally, panting heavily, I dared look over at him.

I saw first the confusion, and then the panic. His face went red.

"No! No!" he cried out. "*Under* the roof!"

I had studied foreign languages all my life, and realized immediately what had happened. He had made a mistake in translating from Danish, wrongly using the word *on* rather than *under*. He had simply meant for me to put the sled under the wide overhang of the barn!

We both collapsed into laughter, me leaning over the sled and he with his arms full of dog harnesses. He had wondered why I had left the packed snow to climb the snow berm. Later, when I told the story to the Kings, Donna and the girls burst out laughing. Jeff stared for a moment in disbelief, and then grinned.

"I do like a dedicated handler."

The handlers—there were three of us—always ate lunch at the Kings' house. There we discussed dogs and kennel chores. We had cooking facilities in our rooms, but often we were invited up to the "big house" for dinner as well. In the evenings, though, conversation centered on Jeff and Donna's three daughters. Ellen was nine, Tessa, fourteen, and Cali, sixteen. The girls included us in their conversations, yet mostly seemed interested in spending time with their parents. Jeff and Donna listened carefully to their stories, and laughed easily at their jokes. I think it often made the rest of us a little homesick for our own families.

Morten was twenty-four and though he had worked before with a Norwegian musher, he had come to Alaska to experience life at an American kennel. Helge was even younger, and I resisted teasing them that I was old enough to be their mother. Shawn Sidelinger, the chief handler, was at least in his thirties, and I immediately knew I could respect his decisions. It was hard to take much direction from the other two. They knew more about dog mushing than I did, but they reminded me too much of my own young fishing crews.

At lunch Jeff told me to take the youngest puppies on a walk while he and Morten ran two teams out on the river. I asked him which direction would be the easiest way to go. For a moment, he just stared at me.

"Down the driveway is probably easiest," he said dryly, "but the easiest way is not always best for the dogs."

What? I thought he had to be kidding. He wasn't and I was too dumbfounded to speak. I certainly wasn't trying to get out of work. I had meant that with all the deep snow—which was the best direction to go. Maybe I had been self-employed too long. I had forgotten the dance steps new employees had to do to prove themselves. He reminded me of some of the skippers on my first fishing jobs, and I bolted from the table before he could see how upset I was.

The puppies and I walked past the house to the edge of a labyrinth of trails in the woods and I forgot about everything else. I had never really dealt with puppies before, and they kept me running. They plunged their tiny noses into everything, chasing whatever moved and rolling in anything that smelled new or different. They were in constant motion, and I never stopped laughing. By the time I got back to the kennel I was totally convinced. I absolutely loved my job. I would find the patience to deal with the boss.

The puppy pen was next to the barn. Inside were several little houses filled with straw, big bones to play with, and a large wheel close to four feet in diameter. It was fastened to an axle that protruded from the wall and worked the same way as a hamster wheel—except that it was built for puppies. Puppies could climb in for a little run any time they felt the desire. Whenever things got too exciting—visitors, teams getting hooked up, birds flying by—they could jump in, start running, and release all that pent-up energy that puppies naturally have. Often the dogs looked to see if you were watching, but I was convinced this wasn't what motivated them. They were just so filled with energy they couldn't help themselves. When I returned them to the pen after our long walk, the smallest one immediately jumped in, quickly joined by another, and together they started racing madly. Sometimes, in the middle of the night, I could hear the wheel spinning and wished David could hear it. He never would have been able to sleep with the wheel spinning; he would have giggled all night long.

On really cold nights, when the temperatures dropped below −20°F, the dogs were given the option to sleep inside the barn. Jeff or one of the handlers would turn on the big yard lights, and the dogs understood. All who wanted to leave the privacy of their little house and sleep indoors just had to let us know. We ran around the yard unclipping anyone who was interested. Many preferred to stay outdoors, but everyone else would charge for the barn. They wagged their whole bodies and wrestled while they waited for us to open the door. It was so comical, yet I had to wonder, weren't they supposed to be snow dogs? How come they loved going indoors so much?

With more than eighty animals at the kennel, I thought it would take forever to learn all their names, and at night made elaborate notes in my journal:

Paris is black as evening velvet, luxurious to touch—a race adult. Pumba is tall and has such wide eyes he always looks surprised. Persian has a polar white coat, coarse and thick with black specks on his ears. Beta is the top dog in the kennel; he is white and barks a lot. Juliet is a yearling, a good leader and delicate like a gray fawn. Jeff named Conan after he went on Late Night with Conan O'Brien. *Cannon, with one brown eye and one gray, does tricks and went to New York City once, riding in a limo to the television studio. She has done several commercials. Dakota was nearly impossible to harness; Morten actually came to help me, though I never stopped laughing at the enthusiasm. Texas is another pup, though I only know where his house is and not really what he looks like. Latte is a white dog in the far back on the left. Eighty dogs, how am I ever going to learn all their names?*

I would write and then study my notes until I fell asleep.

One morning I was horrified to find I could hardly crawl out of bed. Back problems were not unknown to me. Generally a couple of aspirin could mask the pain and I could quickly forget about it—but this time the sharpness of my body cramping took my breath away. I felt totally betrayed, and yet I was scared, as well as angry. After just arriving, I knew if anyone saw me hobbling around, they would form an image—old lady—that would be hard to shake. The guys all seemed so old-fashioned and polite; I knew this would mean they would likely curtail, out of kindness, some of my activities—like hauling heavy loads or dealing with the bigger dogs. Maybe I wouldn't even get a chance to drive a dog team—ever.

I kept my snowsuit in the feed room and started going to work extra early so no one would see me trying to get it on. Mornings were the worst. I worried when Shawn questioned why I hesitated to fill the buckets totally full of dog food, or why sometimes I walked so slowly. I knew how I would feel back in Kodiak if someone as new as me would complain of a sore back from fishing: there would be no sympathy. I kept imagining Jeff and Donna politely telling me I should probably just leave.

The boys were so limber—Morten and Helge often did handstands in the yard. They could lift the heaviest dogs into the truck or carry a fifty-pound bag of dog food with very little effort. I felt old and crippled. I kept getting up even earlier, so that I could stretch and stretch. I also needed plenty of time for the drugs to take effect before anybody saw me. Since I didn't have a telephone in my room, there was no private place for me to call anyone and tell them how miserable I was. I was too afraid someone would overhear the conversation and it would get back to the Kings.

It was easy to forget about my back when I was alone with the dogs. Litters of puppies were named with themes, and this made it much easier to learn who was related. Pumba and Zazu were part of the *Lion King* litter; Piglet and Eeyore were brothers from *Winnie the Pooh*; Mozart was a sister to Chopin, Shuman, Beethoven, and Handel. Romeo, good-looking and so debonair, was one of the movie stars, along with Alberta, Vicky, Juliet, and Demi. Moose was also a part of that litter, but as a puppy had been so clumsy that a stellar name didn't seem appropriate.

One afternoon, when it had warmed up to –17 °F, we were told to hitch up some older puppies so Morten could take them for a run. He and I were harnessing the last one when the team pulled the anchor free and took off racing down the driveway by themselves. Morten immediately chased after them, but in several steps I knew I should get motorized help, and ran to get Jeff.

We jumped into the red pickup and hurried down the driveway—silent except me telling him how many dogs were missing. I was thankful to have answers to his questions and just as we turned right onto the frontage road, the team came running from that direction. They looked great, stretched out cruising with giant grins on their faces. They didn't seem to miss having a musher on the sled at all.

"Good dogs! Come on, Booster—good boy!" I was surprised Jeff didn't seem angry; actually he sounded thrilled to see them. The leaders immediately turned, diving into deep snow and dragging the whole team with them. They acted delighted to see the boss.

Jeff told me I could take the team home, so I nervously stepped onto the sled. I tried to appear confident, but secretly prayed my back could handle the ride. It was a little intimidating with a three-time Iditarod champion following me, but everything went great. I even used the correct command going into the yard—silently practicing for several minutes before arriving.

"Haw, haw."

They felt like silly words to say out loud, and even though I knew there were experienced lead dogs up front, I was still surprised when they suddenly turned left. I tried to hide the size of my grin as I carefully stomped the hook into the snow. It had been unexpectedly easy.

Sled dogs don't learn many commands. "Sit," "Heel," and "Roll over" would never be part of their vocabulary. Generally they are taught "Haw," which means turn left, and "Gee" which means turn right. The term "Mush" is no longer used, but "Let's go" or "Hike!" is music to their ears. "Whoa" is always the hardest to teach because it goes against what they most love to do—run. The animals work so closely together everyone must know the commands—not just the leaders—so that literally it is teamwork that makes changes of direction possible with a forty-foot-long string of dogs.

One of my jobs was massaging Jenna's front wrist with Algerval, an expensive liniment from France. It was easiest if I crawled into one of the short stalls with the little dog, but I always had to make sure no one was around. Shimmying through the door wasn't pretty, and I could never seem to stop a few involuntary yelps.

Jenna was Queen of the Yard. She helped Jeff win the 1998 Iditarod and was obviously different from her peers. When everyone barked in wild abandon over dinner or a loose dog or a sled that was getting set up for a run, often I found Jenna sitting regally atop her little house, knowing and calm. When I rubbed her down, she stared deep into my eyes, occasionally giving the most delicate kisses. Several times I whispered that it was her turn, that I could use a little Algerval on my back as well. Watching her expressions, I became convinced she knew what I meant. She just didn't have a means of reciprocating.

Some nights I could hardly sleep, and desperately missed David. I imagined he was staying up late, working on projects until exhaustion forced him to bed. I knew the house would probably be very clean and he would eat spaghetti every night. He wouldn't be miserable without me, but he would be lonely. At times I was lonely, too, though mostly just at night since my days were so busy.

One morning while I was massaging Jenna, Jeff tried to fire me. He marched into the barn, obviously a man with a mission.

"I've heard you are unhappy," he said. I had been humming into Jenna's ear as I worked, so it took me a moment to get my bearings. He continued, very quietly, very evenly.

"I warned you in December that I was not going to allow you to drive my dogs until I was totally confident in your abilities."

I was totally shocked. *What?*

"I've heard you are complaining about not mushing. I thought I made it fairly clear that there would be very little time in January for teaching someone as green as you are how to mush dogs."

I shifted slightly, biting my lip to keep from crying out. My body had stiffened as I massaged the dog and now I could hardly move. Jeff seemed to note my expression and quickly stood up. He hesitated by the door before leaving the room.

"If you aren't happy with the way things are here—then you need to just leave."

Leave? I certainly wasn't ready to leave, nor did I realize that I appeared so miserable. Secretly I wondered if everyone confused the grimaces I made because of the pain in my back. Did I really look that unhappy? It was almost funny in a twisted way, but there was no way to share the joke without revealing my plight. I imagined David laughing at the irony and tears blurred my eyes. I promised myself to take more drugs, and frequently smile. I also decided to pretend the conversation had never taken place.

CHAPTER 4

Bootie Duty and Other Chores

"You can work indoors today," said Jeff one morning. I smiled wryly. Good idea. The temperature was –40°F. An ice fog hung over the kennel, and the snow squeaked loudly as I walked across the yard, each step echoing longer than the movement itself. I could hear trucks braking a mile away. At –40° everything was exaggerated—the pain of a bruise, the pleasure of a hot cup of coffee. At –42° you could toss the remnants of that coffee high into the air, and it would float to the ground in crystals. Oceans froze, trees cracked, steel snapped, I was delighted to work inside.

I was given the job of sorting Iditarod drop bags. Each musher shipped nearly two thousand pounds of supplies in bags sent out to all the checkpoints. Filled with dog food, people food, booties, and spare parts for the sled, the bags just didn't seem to hold enough for such a big journey.

Each bag had the name of the checkpoint stamped on the side, yet I was embarrassed that I didn't remember the sequential order of the stops. "Of course you know them!" Jeff said briskly as he quickly flipped the bags into separate piles. I didn't know their exact sequence in the race, but the names thrilled me. I dared to ask only a few questions at a time, but Jeff actually seemed to enjoy answering them. *What does Ruby look like? Is Ophir a ghost town? Does the wind always blow in Unalakleet?*

Finally, once again, I got to drive another puppy team. Helge first drove them down the big hill, while I followed with the snow machine. Then he gave me the team. Cannon was the adult leader, and the four puppies seemed to mimic her moves. They weren't very big, just over thirty pounds, but they pulled hard and seemed as serious as the race adults. I was thrilled and hoped it would mean I could really start driving dog teams, but I kept quiet. I certainly didn't want to get fired now.

Several thousand dog booties were hauled into my room. Assembling and organizing things for food drop had to be done by mid-February, and everyone else seemed to have lots of dogs to run. New booties, or socks as I had first called them, needed to be turned right side out, and then folded into sets of four. These were then bagged into groups of sixteen so that there were enough for everyone to get new booties whenever Jeff opened a fresh bag. Booties wore out on tough terrain or got wet in slushy overflow, and from the size of the boxes in my room, he changed them often.

Often I would help hook up the teams and then stand with the dogs left behind as everyone departed on their grand adventures. We would howl together, feeling sorry for ourselves; then I would go back to my chores. Left behind with me was Kitty, a retired champion. She was free to roam the yard as she pleased, gracefully living out her golden years. Her thin white coat reminded me of the translucent skin of my great-aunts. Framed pictures of her as a young dog charging in Jeff's teams decorated the walls and I tried to imagine her ever moving so fast. We never actually consoled each other. It was more like two crabby old women pacing the yard. I whined out loud, but if she ever did, she never let me hear.

One morning my patience was rewarded, and Helge took me six miles out the Ravine Creek Trail with a small team of adult dogs. We flew out of the yard, across Goose Lake, and then down into the woods. The trail wove in and out of the trees and down a hill so steep I wanted to cry out. I really wished I could stop for just a moment to catch my breath, but of course we couldn't. The dogs are so excited at the beginning of the run that it is almost physically impossible to stop them. It was thrilling, yet equally frightening, as I learned to physically control the sled.

It was hard for me to keep my bearings. I was concentrating on not falling off the sled, but when I remembered to look, I loved what I saw. We crossed meadows of open tundra, and skirted several frozen lakes, darting in and out of woods. The faint outlines of tall peaks in the distance edging the valley gave me goose bumps. The alpine glow of the evening was exactly what I had seen for years in Alaska paintings. This time, though, I was charging through it with a dog team.

I loved the cold nights. It was so fun to watch the antics of the dogs scrambling for the slumber parties. Some dogs always wanted to sleep with their best friends and I wondered what had made the bonds. Jenna and Red searched each other out, and I knew together they had once led Jeff through a blizzard outside of Nome. Jody, Alberta, and Demi, three talented sisters whose drive far outweighed their tiny sizes, also preferred to bunk together. No one ever shared a stall with Kitty, not even her offspring.

The days sped by. There was so much to do before the Iditarod; we often worked long after dinner. Sleds were rebuilt, meat was cut into snack-sized pieces, harnesses were repaired, and always there were the booties. No one seemed to mind the long hours, and the pay—simply getting to run sled dogs—seemed like a bargain. Once again I marveled at the energy of volunteers and wished I could use the philosophy in my fishing operation. My salmon crews were making good money, yet nothing seemed to match the zeal of those of us working for free.

From the back of a dogsled, everything looked like an enchanting winter fantasy. Tracks of rabbit, moose, and caribou dappled the white fields disappearing just out of reach of the trail. The trees bent so heavy with snow, I expected elves. The rhythms of the sled, swaying to the subtle changes in the trail, felt like gentle dancing, and I swung my hips on every curve. Except for the excited yelps of the team, and the sled runners gliding, the world was silent. I always came home totally inspired and energized, attacking the box of booties with renewed vigor, hoping someone would want to go out again soon.

It was interesting to work so closely with a "celebrity." If we traveled anywhere, people often stared or asked for autographs. Jeff was a good public speaker and told great stories, though strangely he was almost shy with individuals. His reputation in the press and among other mushers was one of an intense competitor, possessing a single focus—winning dog races—and yet at home, family came first. He expected perfection out of his handlers, but his girls could do no wrong. It was only when Donna or his daughters were nearby that he seemed to relax at all, stopping to marvel when they spoke, reaching out to briefly touch them as they walked by.

One morning I was told to dress warmly. I was going on a long training run with the race team. We loaded fourteen dogs into the truck and drove north for an hour to the beginning of the Rex Trail. Since Jeff was never going to allow me to drive these particular dogs by myself, I was to ride on a second sled tied directly behind his. It was purple and looked like a toy, something a child would play on. As we began to hook up, the dogs turned into lunatics—slamming against their harnesses so the lines threatened to snap, barking so furiously I started panicking. My little sled was looking more and more fragile. When we were finally ready to go, and the slipknot that held the team to the truck was pulled, we pitched forward and were immediately airborne. I clung to my flimsy vessel with all my strength, and tried not to close my eyes. I imagined a turbo booster, even smelled the trail of smoke. This was definitely not the mix of puppies and trainees I had experienced before.

At the first *Gee!* (right) turn, there was a moment of confusion. The leaders plunged into deep snow to get us back onto the trail, but tangled in the turn. Jeff yelled at me to hold the team while he ran ahead to straighten out the lines and I put all my weight on the brake against fourteen muscled machines. It seemed impossible to hold them back and just as I lost control, Jeff jumped back onto his sled. I was relieved he made it; I never would have survived going down the trail alone with such powerful maniacs.

For no apparent reason, my sled then flipped on its side. Immediately I was dragged along with my arms stretched fully in front of me, my face plowing through the snow. It didn't hurt and I almost started laughing, but I knew Jeff wouldn't find it very funny. He had lectured me in the truck about getting knocked off the sled; I wasn't allowed to get embarrassed or bummed out. Ego simply could not get in the way, nor did I suppose, humor. When he finally got the team stopped, I dove back onto my sled without a word.

We traveled thirty miles east to an old trapper cabin, following a timeworn gold mining trail now used by dog mushers and snow machines. It was obvious the trapper hadn't been around for a while and squirrels were the primary residents. A fire in the old barrel stove quickly warmed the cabin and in the shadows of a dusty shelf, we even found crackers and sugar for our thermos of coffee.

Built of hand-hewn logs, our rest stop was like many cabins built to shelter a trapper on his rounds, or traveler on their journey. It was small, and I hit my head on the door frame every time I entered. I wondered if the builder was really that short or was the place designed to some Bush Code unknown to me. The snow reached almost to the eaves, and the spruce trees scented the yard like Christmas. I was told there was a river nearby, not yet frozen enough to cross, but later in the season we would train farther down the trail. This news almost made me dizzy. *What was the country like over there? Were there people? Wolves? Herds of caribou?* Secretly I vowed to finish the dog booties as soon as I got home.

Jeff was relaxed on the back of the sled and told stories as we mushed the thirty miles back to the truck. I heard about Deer—whose mother was Kitty—and how he put the big dog in lead hoping the bloodline would show through. He told me about Red, who had been a late bloomer, and a bit of a surprise when he put him into lead in the blizzard of '98 and won the Iditarod. I learned that if a dog looked back at the driver, either something was wrong or he just wasn't concentrating. I learned how some dogs, veterans like Persian and Moaner, always started out slow, but would increase their effort later in the run when it was needed more.

In the final miles of the run, Jeff went silent. Suddenly I no longer existed, and he was alone with the dogs. His gaze never strayed from the movements of their bodies. He no longer looked at the scenery or pointed out the animal tracks. It was pure business. Back at the truck, we took the harnesses off, loading the dogs and driving the hour home without speaking another word. I assumed he was analyzing the performance of each of the dogs and stayed quiet. I was surprised at how exhausted I was. Riding the sled for so many hours was much more work than I had imagined.

At the end of the month, we drove south for the Tustumena 200, a race that ran through the Caribou Hills on the Kenai Peninsula. Jeff was the first musher into the halfway point, followed closely by a local musher, Paul Gebhardt. They had a mandatory six-hour layover, but there was very little I was allowed to do. Mushers cannot receive any outside assistance during a race, so I couldn't help feed or rub the dogs' feet or even fluff their straw. The only thing I could do was sit near the sleeping team and wait for Jeff to wake up.

The boss had told me to wake him at five o'clock, which would give him an hour to get his team ready to leave at his appointed 6:00 A.M. departure time. I set an alarm in my pocket, as I always did working for the Iditarod, and at precisely the correct time I opened the door to the room where he lay sleeping.

"Jeff. Time to get up."

He mumbled something, and I hurried back to the dogs. Several minutes went by, but he didn't appear in the dog lot. I made myself wait, studying the rows of sleeping teams, trying to learn something. The hint of color in the sky was spreading and the lights in the parking lot beginning to fade when I finally sprinted back up to his room. The room was dark and I was surprised to find Jeff still in bed.

"Good morning Jeff. It is ten minutes after five!" I forced myself to sound gay and chipper. "Are you getting up?"

He peered at his watch, but I didn't expect much of an answer. I quickly left the room. Romeo was barking at someone in the next team, and I pulled him back into his place in the straw, stroking his head to calm him. I saw that Paul had finished feeding his team and appeared to be packing his sled. He had come in just minutes after Jeff, which would mean they would leave close to the same time. I looked at my clock. Twenty minutes had gone by.

I ran back to his room, barging through the door without knocking. I was shocked to find Jeff still in bed. I roughly shook his shoulder.

"Jeff! It is now five-thirty! This is the third time I have tried waking you!" He sat up slowly and rubbed his face with both hands. I no longer cared if I was polite or sounded cheerful. Flipping on all the lights in the room and opening the door to the hallway, I turned a last time.

"Can I trust you to stay up?"

Tilting his head he looked puzzled, but finally nodded. Disappointed, I hurried back down the stairs and out to the team who now seemed fully awake. What was going on? Mr. King had won lots of dog races in his career—in fact he was known as "one of the winningest mushers of all time." Was it over? Was I working for some kind of loser who couldn't even get himself out of bed?

Paul was staying busy—calm, but hurrying. Jeff finally appeared and I was relieved to see him immediately start moving along his team. He barely acknowledged my presence, so I stepped back into the shadows of the building. I wanted the team now to forget about me; it was time to go to work. And in the next forty minutes I saw what made a champion.

The boss did indeed know what he was doing. He never seemed to hurry, and yet he was never in one place more than a few seconds. Every move had at least two purposes; if he was feeding one dog then another was getting his ears rubbed. If he walked back to his sled for more ointment or another bootie, he picked up garbage as he went.

I never saw him break stride, and often saw him stop to pat a dog, rubbing their face or massaging their shoulders for a moment. "Wish me luck," he said as he pulled out to the restart area, relaxed and calm. Then he was off—on time and in complete control. I shook my head. I realized Jeff had rested as long as possible. He had known to the exact minute how long it would take to prepare the team to leave. Paul left soon afterward, on time as well, though he was still closing the zipper to his sled bag as the team shot out of the starting chute.

Jeff won, though he and Paul had traveled together through a terrible blizzard for hours. After crossing the finish line he drove the team up to the truck; there he stopped to pet each dog, murmuring to them as he worked his way to the front of the team. He then lay down next to the leader, a little girl named Peg, and put an arm across her back, his face inches from hers. They lay quietly, sharing the pocket of warm air between their bodies for several minutes. I stepped back and turned to a small crowd of well-wishers who had followed the team over from the finish line. They peered past me, their chatter dying off. Our eyes met, but no one spoke. When Jeff finally stood up, the first words of congratulation came in soft murmurs.

With the wet, heavy snowfall, several avalanches fell, closing off the highway south of Anchorage. One person was killed, and hundreds, including us, were stranded. Our host family, who had invited us to stay for one night, ended up with an entire sled-dog team living in the driveway of their suburban home for nearly a week. We kept busy by visiting schools, explaining to the kids about mushing and the Iditarod. I was amazed how calm the dogs remained as a hundred children crowded close to pet them. One morning a teacher pointed at Deer and whined, "Oh that one looks mean!"

As one of our biggest dogs, Deer indeed did look more like a wolf, more Hollywood Yukon Jack sled doggy, than any of the other huskies. I had to smile though upon hearing this woman's comment, and walked over to him. I threw my leg over his wide back and ran my hand along his nose, across his head and down his neck to his shoulders. His reaction was exactly like that of a cat—he closed his eyes, stretched, and did everything but purr. As I stroked him I looked over at the teacher.

"This one's name is Deer. I spell it D-e-a-r."

The kids nearest the woman giggled and started crowding close to the big dog. Almost immediately his body was covered with little hands stroking his thick fur and I had to hide my smile. I saw the teacher stretching her hand forward, past the shoulders of her students, just to reach his silky ears.

By the time I got back to Denali Park everyone was in the final stages of packing the Iditarod food drop bags. Morten and I made hundreds of meatballs from liver and chicken fat. For hours every day we cut and packaged a variety of meats that would be served as snacks along the trail.

The final sets of booties were assembled and I gratefully hauled the empty box from my room.

One morning, a week or so before the Iditarod, I looked out my window and saw Jeff in the early dawn preparing a sled to take out a team. It wasn't yet quite six and I knew it hadn't been discussed with the crew. I quickly dressed and grabbed a snow machine to scare any moose off the trail. Having them meet a moose this close to race time would have been disastrous.

The moon was just setting across the Yanert Valley, the morning light kissing the tip-tops of the mountains as we headed out. There had been a tension building at the kennel as the big day approached, and we had all trod warily when Jeff was around. Donna had warned us of these days; everything we did, we did very carefully. Most nights I slept fitfully, frequently checking on the dogs in the yard. We were all very proud to have a hand at getting these athletes into the Iditarod and didn't want anything to go wrong now.

Jeff and I went twenty miles or so that morning. When we stopped to snack the dogs, he gazed at the team adoringly. As soon as they finished their treats they were slamming into their harnesses, screaming to go with such complete abandon it made me laugh. Finally he nodded over at me with the first smile in days.

"They look so great!"

The "A" team was ready to race.

CHAPTER 5

Return to the Emerald Isle

*H*elping Jeff's team at the start of the 2000 Iditarod was followed by two exhilarating weeks working as a volunteer in Nikolai and Shaktoolik. It was hard not to touch our team when they pulled into the checkpoints; my arms ached to pet Jenna and Grace, but the rules forbid outside assistance. It was an exciting finish with Jeff just five minutes ahead of Ramy Brooks leaving Safety, but he secured a solid third-place finish over the last twenty-two miles. I was proud of the team, and totally exhausted by the time the Iditarod was over.

I returned to Denali and packed up my little room. David helped haul my boxes to our truck, talking of boats and the upcoming salmon season. Spring had arrived up north while we were gone, and with the long days came a sun so strong that I hid behind dark glasses. It had turned the snowy trails into icy paths that led to where we used to go, and by late March even these were rapidly disappearing. I felt like just a visitor at the kennel; it was time for me to go home. Before pulling out onto the highway, my head was spinning though. *Had the puppies been walked? Was the meat thawing for tomorrow? Had someone replaced the broken latch on the dog truck?*

Uganik was more beautiful than I had remembered, our house an absolute luxury with its windows looking down onto the sea. Spring herring filled the bay, and with them came all the creatures that fed upon the immense schools. I watched fin, sei, and killer whales from my kitchen window. Bald eagles gathered in the cottonwood trees behind the house, darkening the skylights as they swooped by on their way to a seafood dinner. At night from my bed, I could hear the belly roars of the Steller sea lions echoing off the shale cliffs.

I had missed David and my neighbors while up north, but now, back home, I found myself restless. I missed the dogs so much, it was almost a physical craving. I was used to going through my days hugging, petting, rubbing, and praising so many animals that now my arms felt limp and useless at my side. Tazi, our pet dog, got extra treats and long walks; David laughed when I came up to him and furiously started scratching his back.

I took long skiff rides, but I couldn't concentrate on the ocean. I kept going back to my journal, my pictures, my books of the snow country up north. If anyone showed the slightest interest, I would try to explain, but it was usually in vain. If no one believed me about the warmth of the cold—how could they have faith that eighty dogs weren't really that many?

Jeff wrote that puppies had been born. In late May, dear Jenna had given birth to four girls and a boy—Modoc, Lassen, Tahoe, Shasta, and Hoopa. She was a wonderful mother. All the puppies were healthy, the right amount of toes, a palette of browns, grays, and one the color of creamed honey. I tacked the photo he sent next to my bed at fish camp and I went fishing. The red salmon were big that June, silver and heavy in the boat. We didn't catch a lot, but we caught enough, and while picking fish out of the nets I dreamed of puppies.

When I heard Joe Redington Sr. had died in his home in Knik, I got into the boat and crossed the bay to see my neighbor Dianne. She had been my main reference for getting a job with Iditarod. She alone in this maritime environment would understand the true significance of whom we had lost. Although I had only met Joe once in Nome, I sensed the great void his passing would mean to Alaskans. It was big country, but a small community when it came to our living idols.

Through years of hard work, Joe Redington Sr. had restored the Iditarod Trail to Alaska. He had spent years convincing the doubters that an annual crossing of the state by dog team would be possible. One of the earliest believers had been the makers of Tang, the orange drink developed for the space program, and through the years, Tang had sponsored his running of the race several times. I had seen the Hollywood-style photos—the team of trusty huskies pausing along the snowy trail with old Joe proudly holding his refreshing glass of Tang. It made me laugh, but in every checkpoint, the neon "orange juice" was still considered one of the essential staples.

"To old Joe," we toasted on that calm June morning in Kodiak. The sea around us perfectly mirrored a rare, blue sky edged dark with luscious vegetation. This paradise was known as the Emerald Isle, but our thoughts were on snow and sled dogs and a treasure one man had brought back to Alaska.

"May the new trail he is following be as exciting as the one he has left for us." We smiled at the delicate ring of our glasses. Our crystal held Tang.

With the last fish of the season came the first brutal storms of the fall. I had always enjoyed these times, grateful to have the boats safely parked and no pressing need to venture out on the water until the seas again behaved, but this year was different. I felt the weight of isolation and was impatient with the pelting rain. I paced the beaches but kept turning north. I craved snow.

I interviewed again with Jeff and Donna. I wasn't sure where this job was going to lead, but I was not yet ready to be satisfied living back on the island. My friends and family had all been questioning me—what exactly was I doing? Scooping dog poop and working so hard for someone else—for free? At times, I felt like a fool. I worried that I was wasting my time, but the draw this northern adventure had for me was more than just a love of dogs and mushing; it was the Kings themselves.

Donna had come to Alaska as a young seasonal worker for Denali National Park. She loved the outdoors, but she also had several degrees in art. Her wildlife paintings were so extraordinary that they were often mistaken for photographs. When her daughters showed an interest in dance, she had started an after-school program that had literally drawn over half the student population—in a community where most of the adults worked for a coal mine! Her love of color and movement and song had changed this remote community of Alaska. She had done some of the choreography for the dance program, but when I had asked how she was qualified, she simply shrugged, "I just naturally absorb some things."

Jeff's approach wasn't as gentle, but had the same results. He didn't absorb so much as attack. He didn't confront problems, he embraced them. The life he and Donna had created together was a complex business of professional racing kennel, tourist facility, philanthropy, and raising a family. Obviously they were highly successful, but it wasn't the big house, paintings in galleries, or winning the Iditarod that intrigued me. It was their attitudes. I had always been dragged kicking and screaming into every challenge instead of facing them with both feet on the ground. I often felt overwhelmed upon hearing the different issues Jeff and Donna tackled on a daily basis, yet they never wavered. The unspoken tenets at their house and at the kennel were never whining over the challenges and never doubting success. Working near this couple made me strive every single day to be better and do more. With them, anything was possible, and I welcomed the news that they wanted me back.

Once again David was supportive of my desires to explore. He had his own multitude of projects to work on at the house and I knew that if left alone, he would happily work into the wee hours of every morning. I often slowed his progress by demanding a hike or a visit with the neighbors. Unfinished projects nagged at him from every corner of our property and he could not rest until he put some order to the chaos. He would visit me periodically in Denali, but would be happily working at home. Often I laughed, wondering if I had moved from the frying pan into the fire.

CHAPTER 6

Back in the Dog Yard

*T*he first morning it took forever to scoop the yard, each enthusiastic greeting erasing the doubts that I had been harboring. The joy was almost physical at being back in the dog yard. Even without a clear goal, I was glad to be back.

Yuksi was the kind of dog you noticed first, even when the whole kennel stood barking at you. Jeff had leased him for two Iditarods, but had finally convinced his young owner to sell the talented young dog. He was the new king, and reigned from the doghouse closest to the barn, the place of honor. Brian, a protégé of Jeff's, had agreed to sell after seeing Jeff charging down Front Street with the dog in lead. Brian's mushing career was not yet developed enough to fully realize the talents of an animal such as Yuksi. For now, the cash offered made more sense; the sale would help convince his fiancée that money did not just flow in one direction with sled dogs.

Attempting to house and feed a whole team of dogs is probably the number-one cause for divorce among a certain group of Alaskans. If both partners don't fully agree that the needs of the dogs must come first— before a better car, before the trip to see the grandparents, before the blue tarp was replaced with a new roof—then there is going to be trouble. Dog teams cost a phenomenal amount of money. A dollar per day could feed a dog, but even "small" dog yards can have twenty-five or so animals, and obviously they are fed seven days a week. Add to this vet bills, yard maintenance, and gear purchases—the resulting figure stunned me. How could anyone afford it?

I thought about this while visiting other kennels around the state. I saw the great sacrifices people were making, not just those who ran or even hoped to run the Iditarod, but anyone who owned sled dogs. The commitment was 365 days a year, and even if you could still afford a vacation, you had to find a sitter who could handle not just a child or two, but a yard full.

Impractical indeed, and yet the price paid was of little importance to nearly everyone I met. I thought wryly of the warning a musher had given me in Rohn. He had lost two wives and gone bankrupt "over the dogs." When I had mentioned looking for a job as a handler, he had looked away.

"Beware of mushers. They will suck you into their addiction."

Though I had returned to the kennel for another season, I'd convinced myself it was not simply the dogs, but the overall picture that drew me. I was certainly old enough not to be worried about changing my whole life to become a musher, even if I did passionately love individual animals.

Kitty was gone by the time I returned. I missed her stiff-legged patrols of the dog yard, blue eyes nearly opaque with cataracts. She had been free to roam and enter the sphere of any dog's domain, never welcomed, yet unquestionably tolerated. I had only known her, at fourteen years old, as a crotchety old woman: too independent to touch, too dignified to coddle.

In 1996, Kitty was nine years old when Jeff got to Safety, the last check-point of the Iditarod Trail. She had led the team most of the way, and they were now alone out front. They were going to win. Jeff could have left her at Safety, she was tired and carrying the extra weight was a needless burden, but instead he loaded her into the sled to ride the last miles into Nome. She didn't like it at all; she wanted to be running out in front of everyone else, but he felt she deserved to be present in the team as they came down Front Street to win.

We handlers watched old videos of past Iditarods and each time a shot of Jeff's team flashed onto the screen, we cried in one voice "Kit-ty!"

We would marvel at how she moved; her leadership skills were legend. Jeff told us the stories with such awe that later, as we tried to herd her back into the barn to sleep at night, no one would ever think of grabbing her collar and forcing her to move faster. She had earned the respect owed to the Queen Mother, and we waited with unquestioning patience.

I was not the only handler to return to Goose Lake Kennels. Morten was now in charge of the young yearlings he had helped harness-break the year before. There was the state litter—Utah, Vermont, Kansas, and a goofy little brown puppy named Texas; there was Jenna's coffee litter; and there were the puppies named after the presidents.

Every summer, tourists visited the kennels at Goose Lake, not to ride in dog sleds, but to see how a professional racing kennel was run. Jeff and Donna had carefully designed a tour that educated visitors not only about dog mushing, but life in rural Alaska as well. Upon arriving, every guest was given the chance to hold sweet-smelling puppies fresh from their cedar beds. The warm feel of a tiny beating heart in their hands and a not-quite-wet nose on their cheeks set the mood and turned just about everyone into a gushing simpleton.

Jeff told stories of meeting Donna on a trail in Denali Park when their dog teams got tangled, about scraping together the money to afford dogs by being a plumber, a contractor, and a truck driver—to winning the Yukon Quest and then the Iditarod. He showed them the design of a sled, and the clothes he wore to stay warm at fifty below.

One morning, as he spoke, the young puppies scampered around the room, busy little souls that occasionally needed diversion when the wrong thing seemed too interesting or tasty. Jeff explained about naming the litters by themes.

"My daughters come up with the subjects," he said. "There was the meat litter—Ham, Sausage, and Bacon—and two cat litters." The tourists snickered. "The mother's name was Kitty, and one group were the domestic cats—Persian, Siamese, Tabby, Manx. And then there were the wild cats—Leopard, Tiger, Panther, and Cougar."

Jeff lifted a small puppy to his chest. "Then there are these guys, named after the presidents—Nixon, Carter, Truman." He pointed to a white fuzzy puppy with a short tail. "His name is Lincoln, but he answers to the name Stumpy!"

A soft squeal from one of the guests turned everyone's eyes toward her. The woman was staring down with horror, her mouth shocked wide. One of the puppies had climbed up her leg, his tiny front paws wrapped tight around her calf, his little backside perceivably undulating. No one knew what to say, until finally Jeff shook his head.

"We call that one Clinton."

CHAPTER 7

More than Gee and Haw

*A*long with Morten, the other winter staff included Virgil, a retired gentleman from Montana, and Aase, an angel from Norway. Virgil moved with an ease that defied his chronological age, and I soon gave up trying to protect him from the heaviest work. Aase was in her mid-twenties, with green eyes and a sweet voice. She spoke in the singsong rhythms of Scandinavians, tones rising and dipping like notes of a toddler's secret whispers. She was a teacher of outdoor skills in Norway, but had come to Alaska to learn about mushing and sled dogs.

She wore wool. She was passionate about wool. Her hands never idled and after a long day of working with the dogs, she picked up needles and wove the balls of yarn she had brought from Norway into socks, mittens, scarves, a hat. A sweater took her nearly two months when time became precious as training peaked. Fifty-mile days, campouts at −20°F, autumn oranges and soft reds, a narrow trace of arctic blue.

"There is nothing better than wool," she said, and loaned me long underwear that I was frightened to put on. It would be buried so deep under all my other layers of clothing! What if it itched? What would I do if thirty miles along some lonely trail I realized that indeed my American perceptions were true? Underwear should not be made of wool!

But I wore it. How does one turn down the request of an angel? And she was right. It was everything she had said it would be—lusciously soft and warm, and I had to agree. Americans had hurried so thoroughly away from natural ingredients that we hadn't bothered to perfect the art of removing the itch from wool; we had simply gone on to synthetic fleece and convinced ourselves nothing could compete.

Aase and I shared a small cabin: two sparse bedrooms with a tiny communal living/kitchen space. I stacked my clothes in piles on the carpet and set up a tiny writing table: a piece of plywood balanced on milk crates. I tried not to think about my luxurious desk at home, my favorite place in the world to sit. The window was so big, so high, bald eagles frequently startled me as they flew by. Often I could tell the species of salmon they carried in their giant claws. The only saving grace to my northern dorm room was Donna's artwork hanging on the walls. When I became homesick I let the paintings calm me. I studied the details she put in her mountain peaks, the care she put into the dogs' positions and the design of light she crafted for each scene. There was so much to learn. I just had to have patience.

No snow. Alaskans all across the state looked up to cloudless skies and wondered what shift had taken place. Was this part of the warming trend that was making the news? For some, it meant delight. Freedom from shoveling driveways, and the roads remained safe and clear. But for a musher, a winter with no snow is like a surfer tormented by a polished sea.

We trained with four-wheeled all-terrain vehicles, a common practice for summer and fall conditioning. The dogs got hooked up in the same configuration, with towline and tugs, except a heavy machine replaced the delicate wings of a sled. Some mushers were adamant about not running the engine, but we trained idling along, the trick being adding just the right amount of resistance. Up and down the rutted trails, my thumb froze with the incremental movements on the throttle, my back threatened to go out again, and at night I stretched and stretched.

There were of course benefits to using the loud and obnoxious machine; it was easy to stop and great for taking out large teams. I was always in control. Even twenty dogs could not dart off with the four-wheeler—darting implied a beauty and grace that a four-stroke engine eliminated. The Honda was practical to condition large teams together;

making it easier to compare progress, reducing the need for drivers skilled at sled handling, and for a long time it was our only choice.

Yet even when the barest of snow fell, Jeff hesitated having Aase and me learn how to handle a sled with his race dogs. One morning, he had us load the dog truck and promised a trip into Denali National Park. Summer visitors to the park traveled on a ninety-mile road that extended into the wilderness core. Though the park was open all winter, as a rule the road was never plowed, so once the fall snows came, entry became restricted to travel by snowshoes, skis, or dog teams. It sounded like a grand adventure, and if we were lucky, we would see Mount McKinley, the tallest mountain in North America.

"You're going to like this," Jeff said as the three of us lifted a heavy wooden sled onto the roof of the dog truck. "This sled came from George Attla, a very famous Native musher from the village of Huslia. It's built heavier and stronger than race sleds, so it can carry lots of gear. It's a freight sled, and this pole is called a gee-pole."

A three-inch-diameter wooden pole was securely lashed along one side of the sled, extending out forward nearly five feet. Jeff could hardly contain his glee, and he grabbed Aase by the shoulders to watch her face light up.

"And you get to ski!"

Norwegians are born on skis. Finding one who doesn't love it is like finding an American who refuses turkey on Thanksgiving. Aase had brought two pairs with her from Norway, but when she offered to get them, Jeff shook his head. Smiling mischievously, he held up a small pair of children's skis.

"You're going to love it," he said.

We drove to the park entrance, unloading the sled and dogs, hooking everybody up in the usual manner. But when I looked for the tug lines to the wheel dogs—the two dogs who ran just in front of the sled—Jeff pulled out the short skis.

"A gee-pole sled was the traditional method for hauling freight into remote locations," he explained, "but instead of standing on the tail runners, the musher skied or snowshoed just in front of the sled. They guided the load by holding the pole with their right hand, thus the name gee-pole. I used one for years for taking supplies up into Denali Park. The skis are hooked to the towline, and they need to be short because you kind of surf them along the trail."

Aase looked delighted, but decided to go on the second round, returning for her camera while we were gone. Reviewing my Southern roots and imagining the power of fourteen dogs, it just didn't sound like *that* great of an idea to me, but I smiled bravely.

"Since we won't have much weight in the sled, one of us still needs to ride on the back and use the brake to slow the team down," Jeff said. Reading my expression he quickly added, "Maybe at first that should be you."

The dogs were crazy to go, smelling a new trail and, I believe, sensing the freedom from the ATV. Jeff attached the skis where normally the last set of dogs were hooked to the tug line, and enlarged the bindings so his winter boots could easily slip on, and more importantly, off. If things got hairy, he explained, he needed the freedom to leap out of the way of the sled.

With a wave to Aase, we catapulted out of the parking lot and onto the park road. Jeff balanced on the skis as we flew along; I gripped the handle bow tightly and kept a boot poised above the brake. If anything went wrong, I needed to stop the sled before it ran over the boss. This was a huge responsibility! This guy had won the Iditarod three times; if I killed him, I would have to leave the state.

It was also my responsibility to maintain the team at whatever speed Jeff chose for the conditioning aspect of the run. Long-distance sled dogs were not trained to run full speed. They needed to be fast, but not burn out on long runs. Thus during training, the speed was varied to develop different muscles, and even attitudes.

Holding the pole for balance, Jeff indicated speed changes with his other hand. Palm up meant lift the brake and let the sled freewheel. Palm down with a slight twitch to the fingers meant to reduce the speed a tiny bit. When the whole hand rapidly went up and down, I knew we were going way too fast. His direction was constant and I couldn't tell if I was really doing something wrong or the conditions were changing. Finally, he signaled me to stop completely, and jumped out of the skis to switch the position of several dogs. I stood with all my weight on top of the brake and pulled up on the sled to increase the resistance. He gleefully touched the dogs as he walked back toward the sled, grinning.

"So are you having fun?" he said, not believing anything in the world could be more fun than this. He didn't wait for an answer, but slipped back into the skis, lifted his hand palm up, and jiggled the pole, gaily calling out.

"All right, boys!"

It was indeed fun, and when I saw a mountain higher than all the rest in the valley, a shiver ran down my back. I recognized the shape of the peak from my favorite Sydney Laurence painting, realizing he must have painted the scene from somewhere nearby. The artist and his wife had spent an entire summer camping in a wall tent as he painted image after image of Mount McKinley. It was 1913. They hauled the canvases to Anchorage, and since there were not yet roads into the Interior, they carried the paintings on their backs.

The dogs looked happy; they stole brief glances at the new countryside, but seemed most excited about simply pulling. They leapt over imagined obstacles in the trail and leaned into their harnesses with cries of delighted impatience. Occasionally I could see the briefest nose to nose between running partners. *Are you having as much fun as I am?*

I too stole brief glances at the countryside, but generally I just stared at the back of Jeff's *anorak*, his billowing windbreaker blocking most of my view of the dogs. Like following a conductor in a symphony, I varied the brake pressure to the subtle changes of his body language. Too fast, too slow, sensing at times impatience from the boss, though I wasn't quite sure. We crested a ridge and were just beginning a long curve down into a river valley when suddenly he started waving madly for me to slow the team down. The snow had been swept away from this part of the road and I was shocked to find us skimming along on the bare asphalt.

The skis tore away from Jeff's feet and for a split second, he was skiing on his boots. I was bearing down with my full weight on the brake, but the carbide bits could not pierce the hard surface. We skidded along like figures in a kids' cartoon, with sparklers attached to the back of the sled. We were nearly airborne; then Jeff hurled himself backwards and into the sled.

For a moment, I marveled at his agility. In the next move, he was up and over the handle bow, then standing beside me on the other sled runner. It was something I couldn't imagine doing standing still, let alone at fifteen, sixteen miles an hour. As he landed, he started cooing. "Easy, boys. E-e-e-easy." He didn't look at me. He focused straight ahead on the charging team. "Easy does it. E-e-easy."

He sounded perfectly calm, but when I caught sight of his expression, the shock silenced my gasp.

"Drag your boot! We gotta slow them down!"

In snow, you could use a toe or heel in addition to the brake to change the speed of the sled, but now that seemed futile. My boot simply bounced along on top of the surface of the road. I simply tried to hang on. My hands ached and I was starting to sweat, but then I saw it. A precious patch of white appeared ahead of us, and with great relief I felt the team slow as the brake and our boots dug into the snow.

For milliseconds. The snow patch was too short to completely stop the team and they slipped right off the far edge before I could completely stop them—and they plunged forward with renewed vigor. Desperately I looked ahead for more patches of white, but the pavement stretched out black before us. I squinted, trying to see down into the shadows of the river valley. *What was that?* I hastily swiped the frost from my lashes with a mitten. Down at the bottom of the hill, I could see where in the shadows the road crossed a bridge. I shoved the hood away from my face so I could see clearer.

Was that gate across the road closed?

"Jeff!" I said. "Something is wrong—I think the gate is shut!" He jerked the sled at that moment and repositioned his boot to take more force.

"Easy. E-e-easy," he called out to the dogs.

We were not slowing down, and if anything, we were gaining momentum. For a second I figured he must know something more than I did, because I felt like we were totally out of control heading toward a brick wall. I couldn't imagine stopping this team. Jeff seemed to be trying hard to slow them down, but his voice was disturbingly serene. He didn't seem to care about my announcement concerning the gate.

"Easy, Yuksi. Easy, boys."

The bridge was fast approaching. I could see how the incline on the far side would naturally slow us down, but I simply could not see how we could make it to the other side. The gate was totally blocking access to the bridge. I knew I was riding with an Iditarod champion, but damn it! I just didn't get it.

"Jeff!" I yelled. "The gate is CLOSED!"

His eyes widened; suddenly I realized he hadn't heard me earlier and now we were just seconds away from slamming into a heavy steel gate.

"We're going to tip the sled over," he said quickly.

I looked at him in horror.

"Hold on tight—but no matter what, duck your head!"

The clearance between the ground and the bottom of the gate looked perhaps three feet high; he had to be kidding. If there had been time to think I would have bailed right then, but before I could react or even say anything, he shouted: "All right . . . NOW!" He hurled his body sideways, tipping the sled over. We must have been going close to twenty miles an hour. The thick padding on my parka softened the blow, but I could instantly hear it ripping. Gripping the handle tightly, I was dragged along on my belly—my arms extended out in front of me like Superman sailing through the air.

I kept slamming into Jeff like laundry flapping in the breeze. It was a miracle neither of us was torn from the sled. Only by craning my neck upward was I able to keep my face out of the gravel. When I peeked, I was glad Jeff seemed to be keeping his eyes open.

I could smell my clothes scorching as they dragged on the asphalt: then smelled burning clutch and remembered a baby-blue Volkswagen Bug and learning to drive on the back roads of Kentucky. I saw the large knobs on the radio and the splits on the vinyl seats. I heard John Denver and clamped my mouth shut to protect my teeth. My father had gone into debt getting me braces and would kill me if I broke my teeth here.

We passed under the gate at a speed I could only guess, but doubt if I would have lived if I had made contact. At the last second, I opened my eyes to see the cold steel zipping by, just inches from my fingers. I cringed, but held on.

"E-e-easy, boys." Jeff's voice was amazingly calm.

A patch of snow blessed the bridge and we ground to a stop.

"Whoa," Jeff said, leaping up to grab the leaders. He pulled them so they were no longer facing forward, then cringing, looked back at me.

"Are you okay?"

I was still lying down with my arms fully extended. I could see bits of stuffing from my jacket escaping where the fabric was shredded. For a moment I was afraid to move. Finally I wiggled my toes and then slowly shook my head. I'm sure he heard my nervous giggle.

"*That* was wild."

After that, we started using the gee-pole sled a lot, although we never returned to the park. The wind consistently blew hardest down the same valleys, so there were areas where the snow was routinely blown off the road. Jeff had suspected the conditions wouldn't be good around the Savage River crossing, but had no idea that they would be so dangerous. We found other places to train, but he did call Park Service and tell them to open the gate, just in case.

We started training on the Rex Trail, nearly an hour and a half drive north of Denali. I had already been on it the previous year, but with no snow at the kennel, it became our second home. After getting permission from the trapper, we seriously mucked out the old log cabin and cut several trees for firewood. Aase and I found candles and a tablecloth, and despite having once dropped a peanut butter sandwich that was never found again in the dark corners, the place was very comfortable.

For weeks we trained with the gee-pole sled out to the cabin and would return the next day. Aase and I took turns going with Jeff. Whoever was not mushing drove the dog truck back to the kennel and returned the following day with another team of dogs. Besides keeping the home front maintained, there was always a list of needed things for the remote camp. More dog food, more people food, always more coffee, and occasionally a bottle of wine. A different maul, oil for the chain saw, extra snaps, and how about a somewhat current newspaper? Jeff spent day after day on the trail, and though our work schedule was brutal, at least every other day Aase and I got home for showers.

Jeff missed his family, and would question us daily—who had we seen, what they were doing? His youngest daughter scrawled him notes, stick figures showing what words could not describe. He put on his glasses, holding the precious pieces of paper dangerously close to the oil lamp, studying every line. They would make him laugh. Donna would send him tidbits of food and news of the other two daughters, who played every team sport available in the Healy school. The only time Jeff forgot about his dog team was when someone mentioned the women of his life and when he finally couldn't stand it any longer, we would all get to go home for a few days.

It was twenty-eight miles to the trapper cabin, and after a few days of going just a wee bit farther, we finally took the plunge, crossed the river and followed the trail to Gold King Creek. Of course, the river was frozen, but the ice flexed with our weight, sounding like the lowest note on a cello. I wanted to hurry across as fast as possible and tried not to dwell on how I even hated cold showers.

We took turns skiing, though with me, when the team was freshest, Jeff always went first. Everyone assumed that growing up in the South meant I had lacked footwear—completely—but even I had to admit, skis were foreign to me. Being nearly forty-one also made me methodical about gaining confidence for balancing on slivers of wood going fifteen miles an hour behind sixteen strong animals. I wanted the dogs tired before I tied myself to them. Frankly, I would have loved a stiff drink before slipping my boots into the bindings.

Skiing for hours behind so many dogs was like the best of all worlds. It was like cross-country skiing without the work, it was like downhill skiing without the crowds, it was like mushing, except so physical you got limber and tired and felt the full effects of the endorphin rush. I learned to relax and flow over the bumps, to lean less on the pole for balance, to forget that I grew up barefoot.

CHAPTER 8

The Puppies and I

*T*here is a saying in the mushing community, found on T-shirts and bumper stickers, often accented with a picture of the tail end of a sled dog; "The view never changes unless you're the lead dog." It's true; mushers don't spend a lot of time watching dogs go down the trail from the front. I quickly realized that even though I knew everybody in the race team, and could easily recognize them by the shape of their noses, the colors of their eyes, the expression on their faces, there was a big difference going down the trail when you were looking at the other end. Suddenly, I felt like I had to learn who was who all over again.

I had to recognize dogs by their tails: hairy tails, stubby tails, brown tails, tails with a different-colored tip. In the beginning, if Jeff called out for me to fix a particular dog in the towline, I checked both ends before I did anything. Many did indeed have distinct tails, or the color of their backsides was so unique it was easy enough to learn who they were, but distance compounded the problem as well. A dog near the front of the team is nearly forty feet away, and from that distance, many subtle tail differences could be lost.

A dog's tail could also be read. By the way that he holds it, you could tell how he felt, not just if he was happy or excited, but to what degree. You could tell when someone was irritated with the dog next to him, or distracted by the dog in front of him. He would carry his tail differently, stiff, pointing skyward or off to the side—up and away from the offender.

Working dogs rarely wagged their tails in complete abandon like pets. Their language was much more complex.

As a successful musher, Jeff was an expert at reading a dog's body language. The tilt of the head, the position of the shoulders, the way a dog stepped past an obstacle or worked next to a buddy—these were the details that showed the progress of our training runs. Conditioning took place with the variation of distances and the types of terrain, but training was a different matter.

Jeff was constantly switching dogs into different positions along the towline. No one stayed in one particular place run after run. He tried different combinations of little girls running in wheel (first pair in front of the sled) and the husky boys running in swing (directly behind the leaders). Nearly everyone got a chance to lead, though obviously some were better than others. The idea was not only to develop every dog's skills, to train them to run anywhere in the team, but to learn where each dog did its absolute best. During a race, that knowledge would be used to its full potential.

Zazu often appeared disinterested when he started a run. Anybody who didn't know him would assume he was not a good sled dog. He played around with his running mate, and rolled like a puppy whenever the team stopped. He didn't seem focused or impassioned enough to go the long haul. Yet, if you knew him well, you understood he was steady and never tired. He always got along with everybody and was actually a very valuable team member. And if you knew his mother, Nickel, you knew his rolling in the snow was a family trait, an endearing habit that had somehow been passed on to her puppies.

Kanga was fast, the ugliest dog in the yard, and always ready to sneer at the other females in the team. Her thin coat was prickly like a doormat, her ears large and almost hairless. She liked running with the boys, or with one of her own pups, or alone out front. If you brought her into the cabin, she became animated like a Chihuahua, darting from bed to chair to door, wagging her whole body. She always pulled hard and Jeff only put her in lead at certain times; her petite body—her huge desire to pull—ran all the big dogs into the ground.

If Jenna had a running partner, she always ran on the left side. It was her favorite position. However, when running, most of the strain on a dog's body is on the outside front leg, the one that lands first with each stride. Jenna always drove so hard her left wrist had weakened through the years, and she was prone to injury; so Jeff preferred she run on the right side, though she resisted with a huge grin. He would stop the sled and run up to switch her position, but by the time he got back to the sled she was always back on the left. Forty feet away, what could he do? Finally, Jeff taught the smart little leader a new command. When she would jump to the wrong side, he would stop the team and call out.

"Jenna—*over!*"

At first, she would just look at him. He would elaborately set the snow hook and slowly start walking toward her. He would call out again, and usually she would then jump over the dog standing next to her, looking back at the boss with that husky grin. This became the game. She followed his commands faithfully, but she always made her point first.

When I sat quietly with Jenna in the barn or at her doghouse, she often stared intently at my face. Her eyes were huge, and her head tilted in tiny increments to the rhythm of the words I spoke to her, but it was clear she had her own questions for me. *What trails do you like best? How is your mother? Have you diversified your investment portfolio?*

Skiing behind a team of dogs allowed me to study them for hours, and my understanding of their personalities blossomed as I saw them perform under stress or face new challenges on the trail. I saw who was brave all the time and who put up a good bluff. I saw them working hard to ignore a pest, or boost the spirits of their running mate. I saw them being lazy or holding back until just when they chose—and then giving over their whole heart and soul to pulling. I learned who ran best in wheel and who was most content just being somewhere in the middle of the group. I learned that coaching a troupe of dogs, to work them as a team, was much more complex, delightfully complex, than I had ever imagined.

Back at the kennel, daily chores were woven around the weft of the training schedule. Morten was able to train his yearlings closer to home on the shorter trails in Denali. Aase and I harness-broke puppies—the Harry Potter litter: Hagrid, Malfoy, Goyle, and Potter; and Kanga's pups: Reno, Portland, Salem, Houston, and Bismarck. They made me laugh with their high jumps and twists, but when we got them moving down the trail, I shook my head in disbelief. I knew sled dogs were born to run, to pull, but to really believe it, I had to see for myself. Out of harness they were just young dogs, goofy and playfully chasing their tails, mindless in their course of direction, but in front of a sled, another instinct took over. Lowering their small heads in concentration, they just naturally pulled.

Goyle was clumsy and lunged with long legs like a young giraffe. Hagrid was as round as he was tall and chewed whatever came within range of his mouth. Potter was sleek and black with the delicate bones of a greyhound. He had trouble figuring out the lines and got hopelessly tangled on every run.

Reno was black-and-white, fluffy and round. He hid in his house until everyone else was hooked up. He crouched until at last the miniature harness was put in place; then leapt like a kangaroo and bayed like an old hound. He never stopped smiling the entire run. Houston's eyes were just crossed enough to make you look twice, and Portland became so excited he would grab anyone else by the harness and shake them as hard as he could.

Let us be off! He seemed to say. *I want to go Now!*

Jenna's pups were slightly older and could go a little farther—on real adventures. At the end of each run, Aase and I chattered about how good they all were. Salem learned *Gee* and *Haw* so quickly I felt foolish gushing about him to Jeff. Often I had the puppy in the cabin. One night I was watching old Iditarod videos on television, and a musher started yelling out commands. Salem, who had been asleep on the floor, jumped to his feet wagging his tail and started barking—he was ready to go.

We took them into the park, giggling at those who got carsick on the short ride from the kennel. It was not a long run; they were still too young to go as far as the Savage River, so we turned around in a frozen slough. They thrived on the new, exciting country, and when they negotiated a nasty patch of overflow for the first time in their lives, I could hardly contain my pride. They were growing up so fast.

One morning I hooked up all the oldest puppies into one team. We often had an older, steady leader we used for training the young dogs—retired race veterans we could trust to have patience with youth. Booster, Rat, and Cannon were the unsung heroes of the dog yard. They patiently let the puppies chew on their ears and lick their faces while we hooked up the team. I liked to run a puppy in lead next to an older dog, so they would know through example that there was never questioning a command: "Gee" always meant right and "Haw" always meant left. However, on this morning I decided I was not taking a puppy trainer and put Lassen in lead by herself.

Lassen had red hair, an oversized grin, and a nose just a fraction too long. Her ears looked short, as if her mom had put curlers in too tight and forgotten to take them out in time. She worked hard and had done so well leading with puppy trainers at her side that I wanted to try her by herself.

I harnessed ten puppies up at their individual houses and then took a long look at the twirling, barking crowd in front of me. The next step was to get these crazy kids hooked up into the towline before someone chewed free, started a friendly fight, or got too tangled. It was definitely a time trial, and I ran as I connected them to the line.

"All right!" I finally called out and for a moment, Lassen looked behind her, obviously shocked.

Nobody but me up here? Wow!

We took off, and I could hear little yelps of excitement as each turn in the trail brought new delight. Modoc was like a small tank: laying down tracks and never looking back. The tip of Tahoe's tail indicated she was not happy running next to Utah so I quickly changed their positions. Portland leapt forward and then sideways toward his neighbor. He was so excited, he didn't care which direction he went.

However, Lassen fascinated me most. She held her head low, concentrating hard. She moved with the exact gait and grace of her famous mother. I saw Jenna in every step, joyfully out front—fast and "power trotting" down the trail. It seemed as if Lassen was in her own world, and I wondered if she had forgotten about all of us behind her.

We rounded a corner, and a sudden flash of wings shadowed the sky as a hawk took flight. We must have surprised him into dropping his prey because a headless hare appeared out of the blue—and fell into Lassen's mouth! It may have landed just in front of her, but I only saw the joyful leap of a child at an Easter egg hunt. I was shocked that she immediately returned to her serious trot. She held the hare high in her mouth and never missed a beat. Her body language expressed everything.

Cool, this is so cool, like, totally awesome!

Eventually I made her drop her prize, which caused a few moments of complete chaos in the team, but soon I had everyone going again. They ran now with even more enthusiasm. *What surprises awaited them down these trails! What fun it was to be sled dogs! How could life get better?*

"Hey, Virgil, a hinge on the barn door doesn't work right."

"Hey, Virgil, do you mind checking the four-wheeler? Reverse is stuck."

"Virgil, could you change the oil in the truck before we leave in the morning?"

Virgil's decision to winter at the kennel, instead of being a snowbird, was a blessing to all of us. Officially he was retired and yet at the kennel he worked constantly. He did all the jobs we never had time to do. He could change a head gasket or fix a drive chain. He found the bolts we were missing and kept the vehicles running. He scooped the yard, and he harnessed the race dogs. He did a little bit of everything and was good at whatever he did.

Often he would drive out to the Rex Trail or the Denali Highway where we would train. He would help unload and harness all the dogs, packing the sleds and guarding that no one chewed anything important before we left. When we started putting the dogs into the towlines, everything moved at a frenetic pace to get them out onto the trail before something went seriously wrong. Virgil was not young, and if something went awry, he could easily get seriously hurt. Working next to a launching rocket could be very dangerous and I feared a broken hip that would end this idyllic retirement of his—yet there was no sweeter face than his after two days out on the trail. He greeted us with warm soups and the questions of someone who knows and cares.

"How did they do? Did Chip chew his harness? Was it cold by the river? Did you see moose?"

We often saw moose, and nearly always, the giant tracks of wolves. We saw northern lights and full moons and heard river ice groan. I tried to explain to my family in Kentucky, to friends in Kodiak, but they could not imagine and preferred to think I was just odd. However, Virgil understood.

Often after a long day I would be heading toward my cabin, see the northern lights flickering green across the night sky, and turn upon hearing his howl of delight from across the dog yard. We would meet in the hot tub, steam freezing crystal patterns in our hair, our laughter rising and falling with the waves of color from the sky above us. The northern lights would dance for us alone and we clapped our wrinkled hands, seeing the same things and knowing how blessed we were. He was my buddy, my daily inspiration.

First thing every morning I would ask Virgil how he was doing. No matter what the hour, no matter what the temperature, he always closed his eyes and smiled. Then putting his arms above his head, and swinging his seventy-year-old butt from side to side he would sing out, "Grrreat!"

As the winter daylight hours began to slowly lengthen, Jeff started dropping hints. Morten was taking his yearling team to Nome this year, who would take next year's? It was hard to believe, but the puppies Aase and I were training would be real sled dogs by the following year, ready perhaps to even cross the state. But would I?

I looked away when the future was mentioned, so many images and questions in my head. Could David tolerate me being gone from home another year? What about my house—didn't I need to finish painting the upstairs and build bookshelves? How about my body—would my back be able to handle crossing the Alaska Range? Could I keep from falling off the sled going down the Dalzell Gorge?

I would sit with Salem in my room, watching him as he slept. He was perfect: the shape of his nose, the curve of his eyebrow, the silky black guard hairs on his back. He would lift a sleepy paw, absently scratching an itch, and I would marvel at this perfection. Really he was still such a puppy. His legs twitched as he ran in secret places, paws dancing across trails I dared to imagine. Would such an innocent creature really be able to take me eleven hundred miles?

On bad days, I thought it was impossible. I was too old and too inexperienced. Since I had started working at the kennel there just had not been much snow for me to learn enough about driving a dog team. On good days, I began to risk dreaming, to imagine the bond I would have with sixteen animals that could take me to Nome. I began to wonder how it would feel, to make my father that proud of me.

Finally, one morning I voiced it aloud. I would sign up for the Denali 300 Sled Dog Race in late March. I would see how I handled myself. I tried to play down that it was a qualifying race for the Iditarod.

CHAPTER 9

300 Miles—in a Day or Two

I never had fantasies about competing in a sled-dog race. The last time I had been in any kind of competition was back home in Kentucky on a horse named Meander—and we hadn't done well! I had run fishing crews long enough to know what sleep deprivation was like, and knew I could handle that part of the race, but I worried about being able to maintain a high level of awareness to care for the twelve dogs I would be driving. I also would be in the public eye because I had King's dogs. What if I shamed the kennel by doing something stupid?

David couldn't make it to the start of the race. He and Dena were driving up to Alaska from California. They were hoping to make it to Paxson—the halfway point—in time to see me during the mandatory rest. It seemed crazy for him to race three thousand miles in a compact pickup just to see me compete in my silly race—but secretly I appreciated his trying. It was 70°F in the desert when they left, but they carried extra blankets for what they knew lay ahead.

The Denali 300 race route followed the Denali Highway, a road connecting the Parks and Richardson Highways. It's a busy, gravel road in the summer, but the snowplows don't maintain it in winter—meaning it's open only to dog teams and snow machine traffic. It was a perfect route for the new race.

The creators of the Denali 300 had come up with an innovative concept and race philosophy. Restricted to amateurs, the race was intended to provide an atmosphere where people could fine-tune their racing skills without the stress of big competition. Mentors were stationed along the trail, and mushers were encouraged to use them as resources. Since most of the drivers were new to mushing, having the race follow a closed road made sense. No one was going to get lost or thrown from his or her sled because of a difficult trail.

Even so, I was still nervous and worried about everything. Twelve dogs were more than I had ever run in a team. They felt powerful and stronger than my ability to stop them. I had found during the last months of running dogs that each trip was always an unpredictable mixture of agony and ecstasy. I had been on many trips that had bordered on just plain terrifying, and only hoped this was not going to turn into one of those.

At 10:30 in the morning my team and I were escorted to the starting chute. Teams left in two-minute intervals and mine accelerated hard at the start. Fairly soon, though, it felt similar to a hundred other training runs, and I had to smile at my worries. After a while I took Nickel out of lead and put Moose up front so I wouldn't burn out my main leader. Nickel was coming into heat, but her primal interest level was not yet very strong. With Moose's enthusiasm, the whole team speeded up its pace. Soon enough, we caught up with another team and I had to make the decision to pass.

Other than teams from our own kennel, I had never passed anyone before—should I smile? Or would that seem arrogant? Passing silently, without some kind of greeting, went against my Southern heritage. I knew the best idea was to charge past as fast as possible, and this I finally did, with a shy wave at the musher.

By afternoon, I reached the Big Su checkpoint. I parked the team in deep snow, tying off the leaders to some brush. I was careful to move Nickel a safe distance from her more "interested" teammates, as she was showing clear signs now of being fully in heat. I knew the order of the chores I needed to do and quickly began boiling water as I peeled off layers of clothes. The snow was deep, yet the sun was so intense that sweat soaked my clothes. I was not sure how long I was going to stay, but knew I had to wait for cooler temperatures before going further.

Jeff and another veteran musher, DeeDee Jonrowe, were nearby and offered advice as I worked. Having placed first and second in the 1998 Iditarod, they were good mentors for the race. She was easy to talk to, and Jeff had just come off coaching his daughter in her first Junior Iditarod. At times though, his advice was a little paternal.

"Remember to go find the checker and introduce yourself," he said. "Don't forget to thank them and drink plenty of water and don't forget to eat."

I had gone for soup and was talking to other mushers when my team started fussing. There was a ripple of murmuring when they began the barking that made me finish my meal in a hurry. DeeDee smiled at me. "I think your team is ready to go," she said. They were straining against the lines by the time I was ready, baying like young fools. DeeDee stood next to me smiling calmly as I finished up my last chores and prepared to mount the rocket.

"Are you ready for this?" she said and I laughed.

"I never know if I am ready for this!"

The team leaped forward, riding off into the sunset—or close enough. It was 4:30 P.M., and I had been at the checkpoint for two and a half hours. The late afternoon sun cast long shadows of the dogs silhouetted in the snow. I rode the runners with my coat open, and kicked like George Attla—one foot on a runner and the other pushing off the ground like a lap swimmer at the edge of the pool. I kicked for the pure joy of it all. The sky turned orange, then pink and finally dissolved into the hollow blue of a northern sunset. I wished unselfishly upon the first twinkling star. The mountains rose steeply on both sides, peaks that matched the fantasies of my youth, and they were all mine.

By nine o'clock I reached the Maclaren Lodge, which lay tucked in the hilly folds just past a cut in the mountains. I quickly gave the dogs a drink of water and passed out snacks, but wanted to wait a couple hours before offering a real meal. Jeff had told me that a dog is not normally interested in eating just coming off a run. I would have more success feeding if I let them rest first.

I dragged my gear down to a tiny cabin, the designated spot for mushers to sleep. The only other person in the room ignored me while I peeled off the outer layers of my outfit and hung my clothes up to dry. He grunted a few times to himself, and suddenly I remembered who he was— the one with the renegade black hair that hung straight down his back. He had looked more like a biker than a musher at the drivers' meeting. I had forgotten his first name.

"How was your run, Mr. . . . Mr. Beebe?" He was unlacing his boots. At the sound of my voice, his head swung up, defensively fast—as if he was used to guarding his back, like there were only specific times when someone called him mister.

At the drivers' meeting someone had whispered to me to stay away from that one, he had the history of a fighter. His voice was gentle though and we talked for a while as we settled into sleeping bags at opposite ends of the small cabin. He chuckled each time I called him Mr. Beebe, but never corrected me.

I slept hard. My alarm went off before the checker came to wake me; somehow two hours had slipped by. I pulled on my bulky gear in a daze. It was snowing, and I fed the dogs the meal of frozen meat I had thawed earlier. The parking area had become crowded with other dog teams while I slept, and it took me a moment to find my sleeping team. Jeff was supposed to be "babysitting," as I had done for him during the Tustumena 200 race, but instead, I found him in the lodge chatting with the pretty blonde.

In 1998, Jeff and DeeDee had competed fiercely for first place in the Iditarod. Though he had eventually won, Jeff had never stopped looking over his shoulder and racing against the lady in the powder-blue parka. Under the burled arch in Nome, they had congratulated each other with exhausted respect. They obviously now enjoyed each other's company, cracking jokes as I tried to force down a piece of dry meat loaf.

My mandatory six-hour rest was up at 2:54 A.M., and I pulled the snow hook right on time. The snow was now falling so hard that once underway, I immediately couldn't see the front of the team. I felt a ripple of insecurity and couldn't decide which way to turn as I was leaving the checkpoint.

Thankfully Mr. Beebe had left only thirty minutes ahead of me and the dogs turned to follow his old trail, mirroring my gut feelings. I eased my foot off the brake just a fraction and we took off into the night. It was very dark but at least now, my headlamp lit up several race stakes and I knew I was on the trail.

Because the Denali Highway had been closed for the entire winter, the accumulated blowing snow had blurred the edges of the road. In some places it had drifted in such a way as to narrow the track to a sled's width. In other places, the wind had created strangely disorienting moguls, like sand dunes, that made my teeth chatter as we bounced along.

Traveling at night in heavy snow, knowing there was no one else nearby on the trail, was a new experience for me. I was alone. My headlamp was bright, but each pair of dogs in the team became a little less clear along the towline toward Nickel. She was just the outline of a dog, more a phantom of someone leading us than anything else.

About an hour later, I came to a strange marking in the trail and Nickel at first wanted to go straight. I stopped her, peering through the darkness at a line of stakes. It was illogical, but they seemed to indicate that the trail turned right. At my hesitation Nickel, always wanting to please, leaped through the deep snow toward this other trail. I stood on the brake with both feet to hold the team as I strained to look in both directions. The snow and darkness kept me from seeing very far. I kept waving my headlamp in hopes of catching the flash of a race stake.

The new trail had more recent snow machine tracks, and finally I could barely make out some dog prints. It went totally against my dead reckoning, so for a moment I hesitated, then finally called out "All right!" to the team. They leapt forward, immediately diving off a rude incline that nearly knocked the handle bow out of my hands. It was now snowing so hard I had no visibility at all, and traveled totally on the faith of a good lead dog.

The doubts grew and my hands began to cramp from squeezing the handle bow. At times, the trail seemed too narrow, too uneven, but with all the heavy blowing snow, hadn't the miles before Maclaren felt like that? I tried to assure myself, and laughed remembering a friend's comment to my worries about the race.

"At least you won't get lost!"

When I saw the first bush, I started talking out loud to myself. I wanted to believe it had been blown there, pinned down by the snow, but I never really believed it. Brush does not grow in the middle of a highway, even if it has been closed all winter. I desperately swept the beam of my headlamp in all directions, hoping against hope for the sighting of a stake. The wooden lathe markers were tipped with reflective tape, and several times snowflakes turned just perfectly, catching my light, catching my breath.

When my sled runners ran over more brush I knew my fate was sealed. As much as I really wanted to just continue on down the trail, to pretend everything was perfectly all right forever, I knew I couldn't. I had definitely lost the trail. I had to turn the team around.

Turning a team of sled dogs around is always difficult. Twelve independent little minds—all of whom want to please and pull and just get back going—can spaghetti the lines in a matter of seconds. Even with great leaders, there is usually a tangle as the dogs leap around in a new direction. In training, I had always tried to find a tree to tie off to. This gave a fraction more control during the unavoidable chaos and an insurance against losing the team.

Here there were no trees, and the snow was deep. I had never turned around a twelve-dog team and could hardly imagine anything but a disaster. I also knew the dogs were too fresh to park and wait for daylight. It so reminded me of fishing when a moorage line breaks or the seas get too wild. Fear becomes such an unaffordable luxury, so I felt strangely calm. I had no choice.

I waited until we came to a wide part of the trail and was heartened to see a snow machine track off to the left. It would give Nickel something to aim for, so I called out "Haw!" She hesitated, but when I called out a second time, she threw herself and thus the whole team into the deep snow. I held on tightly to the handle bow and tried to shine my light ahead of the dogs while I searched for firmer footing with my boot. The moment I saw Nickel reach a faint cross-track, I once again yelled out for her to haw. My toe found a bit of brush and I shoved the sled with all my might. I called out a second time and my dear, dear leader turned.

We followed this track a short way. Again, I had to command her to leave the trail and jump into the deep snow. Here Nickel finally balked, her blue eyes glowing in the darkness as she questioned what I wanted. Suddenly she started to head back directly toward me—bringing all twelve dogs with her! Instantly I bailed from the sled and dove through the snow.

In the darkness, the messy knot of dogs that was about to be created would have been horrible. Quickly I screamed out "No!" but by the time I reached her, the whole team had just started to turn. I grabbed her harness and quickly dragged everybody back into the right direction. A few long minutes later, I was relieved to see the familiar reflection of the trail stake.

The snowdrifts were often so deep, the dogs seemed to be swimming rather than running on the trail. Only the race stakes comforted me, and I obsessively searched for each succeeding reflector. At Mile 43, it was just light enough for me to see down a side trail. Prints in the snow showed where a team had recently traveled, and I guessed that Mr. Beebe had also taken the wrong trail.

Gradually the sky lightened, and the snow lessened. We climbed and then slid down the hills just outside Paxson. The dogs looked great, but the mandatory eight-hour rest was going to be good for all of us. Moose was still slamming his harness and Ice was still playfully fooling around whenever I stopped, but Peña had lost some of the spring to her step, and Beta had far more patience than normal.

A few miles out of town, I was surprised to come around a corner and find David on a snow machine next to Jeff. He and Dena had somehow made it all the way from southern California to Alaska! We waved greetings, but I continued by them without stopping. Even if these hills were slowing me down, I was still in a race.

The dogs curled up into their straw nests when I reached the checkpoint, and I covered them with blankets. Although their feet looked fine, I rubbed the French liniment between their toes and massaged their pads. It was for mental as much as physical reasons, all of us equally enjoying the sweet-smelling chore. Later David bought me eggs and hash browns while Jeff grilled me on how each team member was doing. *Was Nickel in heat causing problems? Was Carter doing his fair share? Did the new dog, Ice, keep up with everyone else?*

Like a true outlaw, Mr. Beebe's first name was Jesse; I had heard his first name spoken at the checkpoint and laughed. He had the polite manners of an old-fashioned bank robber—tipping his hat and talking real soft to the ladies, but staring the men down with the ability to peel paint with his eyes. He had a very good team and was still ahead of me—but my dogs were electric after we pulled out of the checkpoint. I started kicking the moment we reached the bottom of the first long hill and together we ran. I grinned to myself; maybe I did have a chance of beating that Mr. Beebe, that rebel from Delta.

CHAPTER 10

Baby Blue Eyes

*I*t was snowing hard and darkness came quickly as I climbed back out of
the hills west of Paxson. I wistfully looked at the dark buildings of a
lodge I passed, now closed for the winter, not feeling particularly thrilled
to be heading into the blackness of the night. The snowflakes crowded the
narrow beam of my headlight, and the trail deepened by the minute.

A long hill meandered down from the lakes into the Maclaren River
valley—fifteen miles of downhill travel. The dogs loved it, and during the
last hour before the checkpoint, we literally flew. Careening off snowdrifts,
I hung on to the handle bow feeling like a blind rag doll. I couldn't see
past Nickel's head and had to keep faith in her ability to follow the trail.
There was no past, no future, and no trail other than what the sled runners
were on at that precise moment. The world had narrowed.

A mile or so out of Maclaren, I came across Jesse Beebe's team parked
alongside the trail. We were moving so fast that I passed without even
acknowledging him, and for a few seconds even debated on whether it had
really happened. Then I realized that, for the first time in the race, we were
in first place. The team seemed to sense the difference and raced even faster
toward Maclaren.

We plunged into the deep powder snow of the parking area for the
checkpoint and I searched for a place to put the dogs. I knew I wouldn't be
around for long, just enough time to snack the dogs, with (hopefully) a
pee and perhaps a cheeseburger for me. A couple hours at the checkpoint

would be plenty. I had just started to get my cooker out of the sled, when Jesse Beebe pulled in behind me. He signed the necessary paperwork, briefly flashing his headlamp along my team and then to my surprise pulled his snow hook and charged right by!

The Susitna checkpoint was forty-three miles farther, probably at least five more hours, and the snowfall assured a difficult trail. Jeff came over to my sled. "It's up to you, but I'd keep on going. You have a mandatory six-hour rest at the Susitna River." He tried to read my expression in the dark. "But it's your decision." I shined my light forward along the team, the dogs were looking back at me for direction.

Then Jeff added, "It *is* a race."

I walked the length of the team to Nickel and gave her a brief hug. "Then I think I'll just keep going," I said to no one in particular. Without another word, I quickly pulled the snow hook before I could dwell on the image of traveling through the snowstorm all night. Wryly I realized bathroom duties would have to be done from the back of the sled, and a granola bar would have to substitute for the cheeseburger.

About a mile down the trail, I found Jesse snacking his team. The trickster! I quickly passed him and then worked hard at gaining some distance between us. The snowdrifts were deep, making traveling difficult. As soon as I could, I stopped the team and pulled out food; they deserved a treat. Quickly I scooped a small pile in front of each dog and just as I got the cooler back into the sled I could see Jesse's light approaching down the trail. I pulled the hook and with a lot of verbal encouragement, we took off.

The dogs were now feeling tired and I sang out to each one individually. I fought to keep my own eyes open and started reciting poetry, naming the states in alphabetical order and running through Christmas songs. For a moment I relaxed, letting the heavy weight of my eyelids pull them down. It felt absolutely delicious, and I'm sure I would have fallen asleep, if a different disaster hadn't struck.

It was probably Vicky who took the first wrong step off the trail and plunged into snow well over her head. I was too slow getting my foot on the brake and, like a collapsing accordion each dog rear-ended the one ahead of them, their lines instantly tangling. I stared, speechless. How could such a disaster happen so quickly, so completely? I adjusted my headlamp then suddenly realized something more was also going on. For a moment the movement puzzled me but then I understood—it was the boys! I had been keeping them in the back of the team away from Nickel, but now in the frenetic fracas they were falling enthusiastically in lust. As they pulled to get closer to her, their tangled lines tightened, making the whole knotted mess increasingly worse.

One of the most fundamental axioms of dog mushing is that the driver is completely responsible for the health and welfare of every dog in the team. If they are hungry, they will be fed; if they are tired, a place for them to rest will be found. If the lines hooked to their harness get tangled—then something will be done before the dogs get hurt.

With the constant forces generated by the rest of the pulling team, a line wrapped around a dog's leg or neck can quickly tighten into a life-threatening condition. Teammates have suffocated and died in tangled lines, or have severely injured themselves in the panic of not being able to move.

I was acutely aware of this responsibility. I quickly threw down my snow hook, stamping it into the deep snow with absolutely no faith that it would hold. I stepped off the packed trail and immediately pitched over as the depth of the snow stopped my forward motion. Righting myself, I started using my arms like pendulums, swimming my way to the front of the team.

Every single dog seemed wrapped in the lines. Some of the girls had simply lain down and seemed content to wait for rescue. Others balanced on their "free" legs, awkwardly holding up the trussed appendage for me to attend to. Vicky and Peña actually seemed to be enjoying the break, nuzzling each other like little sisters.

Moose and Ice had other things on their minds. Both were politely and purposefully working their way toward the front of the tangle. Nickel seemed to be smiling, and like a teenage prom queen, looked at the boys, coquettishly batting her baby blue eyes, her tail held high. They wanted her and she wanted them. She was truly a bitch in heat.

There are many reasons why you don't want dogs to breed during a race. One is that it takes quite a bit of time, and the race comes to a complete halt until the date is over. Another, and the one that I was most concerned about, is that in a modern racing kennel, any normal breeding is a carefully planned event. Competitive kennels like Jeff's can track certain traits back through the lineage of their dogs for generations. A valuable dog such as Nickel would only be coupled with a worthy male whose desirable characteristics had been found genetically transferable. Jeff would be at best furious if I let Nickel be indiscriminately bred, or worse, very disappointed.

I reached into the canine morass and dragged my sulky girlfriend up and then down the trail a short way, anchoring her in front of the team. As I began the tedious job of unraveling the knot of dogs, I marveled at how patient they each were, waiting in turn for me to free them from lines that were often tightly wrapped around their legs. As the ball unraveled, I moved Nickel farther down the trail allowing instinct to stretch out the team toward her.

Sweat soaked my beaver hat and my arms grew numb with exhaustion from all the lifting. I was no longer the least bit sleepy. Finally I saw that everyone was free, and for a split second they looked good, lined out and ready to go. Then Moose began barking and the snow hook gave again. Before I could finish wailing "No-o-o!" the dogs were surging forward into a living mass on top of Nickel, on top of me. It only took seconds.

I wanted to lie down in the snow. I wanted my mother. I wanted a blanket to cover my head. I wanted to take a nap and dream of a place far away. Then I realized several of the dogs were looking at me, their eyes shining in the beam of my headlamp. No one was panicking; they had faith that I would come forward again and untangle the chaos. They trusted me, and with this trust I took a deep breath and moved before the tears could come.

I reached the Big Su checkpoint at 3:30 in the morning with a weird feeling that Beebe's team had burned the last of their fire. The checkpoint was the last mandatory rest of the race, and by 9:30 the next morning, we were again heading out alone onto the trail. I ran as much as I could alongside the sled, and Moose wagged his tail at me in encouragement. Vicky was now coming into heat as well, and with the girls in lead, there was a delightful chemistry in the team. It didn't surprise me that we didn't share the trail with the Rebel.

What I feared most was the heat that invariably comes in the middle of the day. As the sun arced overhead and grew stronger, the dogs began to wander on the trail, moving slower and slower. Thirty miles from the finish line, I shut the team down for a nap. It was a risk, but it was just too hot to continue. I only hoped the teams behind me were also enjoying the warmth of this beautiful sunny day—and needing a siesta as well.

I laid my head down on Nickel's back and after murmuring sweet things into her ears, closed my eyes. I wanted to bond with her. I wanted her to know I was tired too, but to love me enough to lead this team again when I asked.

I fell sound asleep, but was surprised to wake up exactly an hour later. Seeing my whole team curled up into such tight little balls sent a ripple of panic through me. Had I made a mistake? I walked back to the sled to dig out a bag of snacks. I knew no one would be interested; it was too hot to eat. It was too hot for anything but a long afternoon nap. This was scary, and my own trembling made my mouth go dry. If this team did not agree that we should get back moving, we could still lose this race, even this close to the finish line.

I started singing, forcing the tune to sound lighthearted. I felt sick to my stomach. I passed out the snacks, which no one looked at. I lifted each dog up, massaging its neck, along the back, rubbing behind the ears. Every single one lay right back down, tightly closing its eyes. By the time I got to the girls up front, I was really starting to panic. Surely another team would show up soon.

I raised my hands above my head and then slowly turned around. Like a Disneyland character I clapped and shuffled in circles on the closed road. My boots kept me from moving fast or gracefully. Finally I saw the briefest, but distinct, movement of several tails. They were faking it! They weren't asleep!

I had heard of using a dog in heat to your advantage, the philosophy being that hormones can give a weary dog team something else to think about. I decided to try it and unhooked Nickel from her tug line.

I started by giving her a nice long back rub right in front of everybody; slowly running my hand from her head to her tail, scratching her back and ears, gently spanking her backside. Then I began parading her up and down the team. Peña and Kaladi of course didn't budge, they couldn't care less, and I think Paris simply cracked an eyelid—but the boys were different.

Ice, being the youngest male on the team, was like a teenaged boy with cheerleaders. He was first on his feet. Wagging his tail, he immediately started pulling on his tug line. Beta stood up, stretched and leaned into his harness to sniff at Nickel as we went by. Moose leapt to his feet and started barking. I risked a smile. It was like magic. My team was waking up.

I let Nickel enjoy her popularity, batting her blue eyes and putting an extra sashay into her strut as we walked the length of the team. I hooked her back into lead position with lots of praise and ran back to the sled. With every ounce of energy left in my body I shoved it forward at the same time I shouted, "Hike!"

The last twenty miles of the race I stopped every half hour or so just to give everyone a pat. When at last I saw the small crowd and the banner marking the end of the race, I was too tired to be nervous.

The dogs were wrapped in loving arms as soon as we stopped, standing proudly, wagging their tails. David and Dena had made it on their own mad dash through the snowstorm and looked as worn out as I felt. I may have just come three hundred miles by dog team through a blizzard, but they had traveled through deserts, freeways, and their own storms to be here. Ellen King, already at home in the winner's circle, proudly stood on the sled runners with me as the race judge looked over my mandatory gear and declared me the winner.

We finished the race in 51 hours and 19 minutes and at some point during the reckoning, I took David's hand.

"I need to do the Iditarod."

CHAPTER 11

Adrift

*A*fter packing away the fishing nets and helping David harvest the last remnants of our garden, I moved back to Denali the following October. I had wrapped fish and venison for the freezer in small packages, portions that David alone could use. Until I was gone, I hated leaving. Everything looked like a watercolor painting, the whitecaps silhouetted against the dark gray of the cliff sides, the bouquet of fall colors from the wild grasses and trees that covered the islands. I moved about this wilderness stage as if in a dream. *Why, why, why?*

David never asked why. Because we had never had children, our life together had been a series of projects and adventures. He knew my restless nature, my need to immerse myself blindly into something new, and mushing was not a surprise. Surely he would have preferred a more maritime passion, but at least it was dogs and still in Alaska. He was resigned to support my decision at an attempt to run the Iditarod. He and Taz would stay in Uganik, but periodically come up for visits throughout the winter.

Until the first snow I was depressed in Denali. *What in the hell was I doing so far from home?* Now as chief handler I at least had my own private cabin, but there was no running water and I hated using a slop bucket for the gray water from the sink. I shared a filthy outhouse with the other handlers and resented that nothing was mine and I had no control. I was forty-two years old, and I missed sitting at my own desk, sitting on my own toilet. We trained with the noisy four-wheelers and I constantly smelled like exhaust.

Then it snowed. The sled dogs stretched in front of their tiny houses and raised their noses to the heavens. Together we watched the fat flakes floating down from the sky, and I knew what they knew. The world changed before our eyes. I saw magic in the face of every single dog and adored each personality with a consuming passion. Finally I spread my arms wide and counted all the blessings that allowed me to be standing in this spot, living this dream.

Every night I had several dogs stay with me in the cabin. Tahoe would stretch out on the floor, raising a leg for me to come rub her belly whenever she caught me watching her. Bismarck came in tiptoeing on the carpet with his tail held high—but he never relaxed, or figured out that peeing must only be done outdoors. Jenna claimed Tazi's fancy dog bed, and lay regally with her huge eyes taking in every detail of the room. She was so elegant, it made me sit up in my chair and pull back my shoulders. It was like a nightly slumber party, but when I needed cheering up, I brought in Jenna's pup, Lassen.

Lassen never stopped moving, and I never stopped laughing. She was like a dog on catnip. It was impossible to get anything else done when she was inside. She stuck her nose into everything, snorting at new smells, hauling miscellaneous items to the carpet. She didn't really chew, though she did do little experiments with taste and texture. At a rapid speed, she explored every square inch she could reach in my little house. Often she would put her front feet up on the couch to check her reflection in the window. Shaking her short ears, she would turn for different profiles, then grin and dart around the room. My bed was built high off the floor, and sometimes in the middle of the night, I would find her standing with her front feet just reaching the edge of my mattress. She didn't want up, she just wanted to see. She was curious about everything.

The first night we took the puppies on an overnight camping trip on the Rex Trail, I was nervous. Jeff and the other handler, Peter, took two teams of adult dogs; I followed with eight of my best puppies. It was much farther than they had ever gone, so I told the guys not to wait for me, nor to worry; I was going to give my young dogs lots of rest on the twenty-eight-mile trip to the trapper cabin. I was a little nervous traveling by myself, but knew the trip would be good for all of us.

They absolutely flew. Rest? They were so strong and enthusiastic I could hardly slow them down. I tried to stop and pass out snacks, but these sled dogs were just crazy about running. I felt a mixture of pride and embarrassment arriving at the cabin so soon after Jeff and Peter. I half expected Jeff to be upset that I hadn't rested the pups along the way, but he stopped working and grinned with delight as the team charged into the woods. They had just run farther than they ever had in their whole lives and looked fantastic.

My team couldn't sleep that night. I had made beds of thick straw among the spruce trees, cooked them a huge dinner with extra meat, and still they were too excited to lie down. They barked when the wind made the branches of the trees whisper, or the river ice groaned from a quarter mile away. Maybe they heard wolves in the low foothills or the whining cry of a barking fox. They just couldn't sleep, and kept calling out to these other creatures of the night. Periodically I would leave the warmth of the cabin to pet each of them and fluff their unused beds. They wanted me to stay; they wanted to play and show me how brave and grown up they were acting. I left laughing, though I peered often out of the cabin window.

Tahoe was the first to try out her bed, then Salem, but both Lassen and Bismarck fell asleep sitting upright. I found their beds in the morning untouched. Jeff warned me, "They'll be tired today," but our speed was only slightly slower than the trip out, and we finished the run feeling pretty proud of ourselves. Their first overnight trip had been a total success. The puppies were growing up. I, on the other hand, was getting more nervous.

The Rex Trail was easy. It was wide and straight. There was the trapper cabin, and another twenty miles beyond that, Gold King. It was a good long trail, an easy way to put in lots of miles with the luxury of a cabin to stay in at night. After nearly three decades of mushing, Jeff did not feel like he had to practice camping. He readily admitted preferring the training runs that incorporated the use of cabins, though I often found him sleeping outside.

Riding on sleds for hours could get boring, but I always concentrated so hard on the dogs that I had to remind myself to look at the scenery. It was easy to forget about the country you were traveling through, but driving a team behind Jeff kept me alert. He often silently pointed out tracks along the trail. I would catch him looking for an extra moment in some direction, and I too would see the bit of color in the cloud, the moose, the wolf tracks as big as hands in the snow. Jeff King loves being outdoors, loves mushing dogs, yet his family is paramount in his life. Our training schedule routinely changed because of a high school sporting event. I gamely attended them, but only vaguely paid attention. It was at these times I most missed my own friends.

One morning when Jeff and Donna were leaving on an overnight mushing trip with the family, Jeff waved me over for last-minute instructions on care of the kennel. The middle daughter, Tessa, had been torn about going on the trip, and had chosen to stay home. For Tessa, a typical teenager, socializing with her friends had seemed more exciting than a cold sled ride—at first—but now after seeing the rest of the family pack, she was having doubts.

"You know there is only one thing more important to me than my dogs," Jeff said, gripping the steering wheel and glancing in the rearview mirror at the house. It was all he needed to say. I fed the dogs, but my true attentions went to Tessa.

By mid-November, both rivers on the Rex Trail were frozen and our dogs were traveling far enough to make training runs all the way out to Gold King—fifty-two miles one way. I looked forward to seeing Larry. He lived on the edge of a ridge overlooking a valley that extended north as far as the eye could see. At night, the stars blanketed the sky until they blended with the backwash of Fairbanks's city lights some fifty miles away. We were always cold and tired by the time we had traveled that far, yet the warmth of Larry's fire and good company was a delight that I always anticipated.

He was a meticulous craftsman, and I loved questioning him about the details of his cabin.

"The table? Oh I made it from a cottonwood tree I cut in the creek bed down below that cabin where you're staying." The wood was a creamy white, sanded smooth, tickling my fingertips as I stole a touch on the way to the platter of moose meat.

He had made the floor, milling the trees himself and then sanding each one to ballroom perfection. The couch and easy chairs were family heirlooms, carried first by pickup and then on a trailer pulled fifty miles by a snow machine. Larry's cabin was always warm and inviting, his company and meals satisfying and delicious.

"I want to come live with you, Larry," I teased him.

Traveling on the back of a dogsled for five hours when the temperature often hovers at $-15\,°F$, $-20\,°F$, or $-30\,°F$ is damned cold business. Thick crusts of ice form wherever your breath meets the chilly air, so neck gaiters freeze stiff, and any escaping bangs soon become encased in hoarfrost. I waved my arms and tried running alongside the sled to circulate warm blood into my extremities, but it certainly didn't always work. There were two things, though, that kept those last frozen hours from becoming unbearable.

Larry had a sauna. Handcrafted out of logs that he carefully chose, the small building was elegant, quite beautiful—and very hot. When he knew we were coming, he lit the fire well in advance. And with this vision forming in my mind, the last miles of the trail flew by. Within a ten-mile radius of Gold King lived several families, and though I never met any of the other local residents, I sensed their presence because I could smell their fires. The familiar aroma teased me that we were getting close to Larry's cabin. It made me salivate, though not just from a hunger for food and good company, but for the thick steamy heat of the sauna. No matter how stiff and frozen I was from the long miles on the trail, I never let it get me down; I knew the evening at Larry's would be worth it.

The other thing that made those last cold miles a dream was what happened with the team during the final half hour of the run. Using a snow machine, Larry had groomed this part of the trail to perfection. It was wide, clear, and as smooth as a path through a city park. It swooped through the woods in gentle curves, past large stands of spruce, cottonwood, and alder. The driving was so easy; I relaxed on the sled and let the magic wash over me.

The dogs also smelled the smoke, and they knew what awaited them as well. Larry had made a row of doghouses for visitors and kept bales of straw to keep them cozy. The overnight accommodations for dog teams were as luxurious as the ones for the musher, and knowing what lay ahead made the dogs concentrate and pull harder. I always let them fly the last miles approaching camp. Knowing the trail was wide and safe, I loved turning off my headlamp and hurtling through the darkness like a ship with the stars and planets speeding overhead. There were times with the moon when it was almost too much, though. Too much beauty combined with the intense cold sometimes made me feel like a reluctant visitor when I stepped back on earth.

The Rex Trail was relatively easy, but I knew it was not what I needed. With so little experience driving a sled through tough terrain, I knew the Iditarod would be a disaster. I definitely needed to learn how to drive a sled better so the section through the Dalzell Gorge wouldn't kill me. I started concentrating on the trails closer to the kennels. Unlike the veteran race-hardened adults, the pups did not get bored doing the same trails that wound through the woods and hills near home. In fact, youth seemed to need the trees and tight turns to keep their interest high. The older dogs could put themselves into a rhythmic trance on the long, straight trips down the Denali Highway or out to Gold King—but to keep the pups happy, I needed to make sure the trips were stimulating.

Steadily I had begun to lose weight as the winter progressed; I had no appetite at all. My stomach churned as I began to play and replay all the scenarios of the disasters that awaited me in March. It made food a sickening thought. Larry nicknamed me "Slim" and I wore long sweaters to cover my hipbones that had grown too sharp, avoiding my jeans that no longer fit. Mornings, every bite of breakfast threatened to come back up, and I counted my chews, gripping the table for support during the act of swallowing.

I was not sick, and obviously I consumed plenty of calories—the job was very physical and I couldn't do it if I were weak. However, getting food into my system became a matter of timing. When I felt calm, I slipped down as much food as I could. I knew that when the waves of fear returned, I would have to function on old calories.

When David called, he would try to reassure me. Of course I could do it. Of course I could run the Iditarod.

"Jeff would not have you running his team if he did not think you could do it," he repeated with such confidence it almost made me angry. He obviously didn't get it! I stopped telling him I was afraid, but secretly hoped he understood when I mentioned the trees I was hitting, the dark purple bruises that dappled my arms and legs. I couldn't explain that the dark circles under my eyes seemed to soften the shock of the black eyes I routinely got. Finally I decided if I never really voiced my fears, maybe they would go away; maybe I would close my eyes and wake up in April, and this whole mess I had gotten myself into would be over. Then I could go home. Then I could be my own boss and even take the day off. I could cook eggs and pancakes. I could eat them without wanting to throw up. I could watch the sun rise above the mountains I loved, and from the kitchen table, see my beloved eagles fishing. I could sleep in my own bed. And I could even sleep through an entire night.

But then the next day I would go on a run with my puppies. I would see one star performer, or two, or the whole team would shine. The sled would behave and the trees would keep their distance. I would feel strong and confident—nothing could stop me.

There were times, going back to my cabin, I would be so jazzed I could hardly walk. I would unclip a bunch of my buddies and race them to the cabin door feeling young, healthy, and strong. We would wrestle on the floor, and the room would be so full of life, good-living life, that I would twirl and laugh in delight. No matter what, I reasoned, it was all worth it just for this.

CHAPTER 12

The Christmas Bash

*D*onna and the girls were in New Zealand that Christmas, and without them around, Jeff refused to acknowledge the holidays. I could sense his strategy—if we all threw ourselves into training so that not a moment lay idle, then we (but especially him, I think) would make it through those celebrated dates. Normally Donna decorated the house elaborately, and the girls wore red velvets, sang carols, and made cookies sprinkled in green. This year however they were still cruising in shorts around New Zealand, and I believe Jeff simply refused to allow Christmas in his thoughts.

The training schedule for December at a racing kennel is always brutal. These are the last weeks of long-distance runs, as January and February are the months of races and almost a period of rest before the Iditarod. So actually, it was easy to ignore the brief snippets of Christmas music we heard in the truck as we drove to the Rex Trail. With no stores or television, we could almost convince ourselves it was not happening because I, too, desperately missed my family.

David was in Uganik. I could picture exactly how the lights were strung in the windows, which favorite Christmas cards now hung along the door, where he had likely placed the candles. A carryover from a time when we had no electricity, I had collected candles, and to celebrate holidays I lit them all.

In Denali, I struggled to tack a few cards on the wall of my cabin. My father sent an artificial tree that came complete with decorations, but the box remained on the floor near my boots. By the time I took my boots off at night, I had no energy to move it.

The Rex Trail, the Denali Highway . . . we were lucky and the river froze so we could train even farther just out of the dog yard. The Horse Trail, the Ridge Trail, the power line . . . we wove patterns between the lakes, the valleys, and nearby hills. I spent hours and hours of nearly every day on the back of a sled.

As the weeks passed, my puppies transformed into dogs before my eyes. Where they had been lithe, thin young dancers on the snow, I could now see their bodies at work as we traveled down the trails. Their shoulders were wider, their backs more defined, and the muscles on their thighs stretched tight under their coats. I found myself humming notes from *The Nutcracker Suite*, mesmerized by the beauty of their little backsides. They reminded me of male dancers in tights.

They wanted to run, and run farther, and then run some more. They got crazier to go. Nearly every day I had moments of such terror that later the smell of sweat in my clothes was that of someone else, something else. The power of the team felt beyond my control, the trees passed faster on both sides of the sled, and an almost constant video of collision after collision played in my head.

But more than anything else, I was afraid of hurting the dogs. If I got knocked off the sled and they went freewheeling down the Dalzell Gorge or some other remote part of the trail, would I be able to save them? Could I live with myself if the dogs got hurt? They trusted me completely; they had faith that I would never bring them to harm. Could I live with myself if I broke this faith?

I did not cry myself to sleep at night, but often when I woke at 3:00 or 4:00—or worse yet, 2:00 A.M.—I hugged my knees and pressed my face into the darkness of my blankets, biting the edge of my hand. I desperately looked for a book I knew that described the Iditarod Trail, but when I found excerpts on the Internet, the adjectives haunted me for days. Don

Bowers's "Trail Notes" routinely warned mushers to "say your prayers and revise your will." When I dared read the descriptions, I usually ended up leaving the computer to lie facedown on the couch.

I kept flipping the sled, hitting the trees, stumps, anything remotely in my way. How would I ever get down the Happy River Steps? Would the Yukon River open up and swallow me whole? What would I do in a coastal blizzard? How would I know when to wait out a storm? Sometimes I had to cry out just to shut up the voice in my head.

Though by no means was every day miserable. The terror came in short stabs, ugly and deep, but often left no marks. At times, it would seem to paralyze me, but in reality I kept moving. I did the chores, I ran the dogs, I made the jokes that agitated Jeff. We trained and trained and suddenly the end of December was just days away.

My dear friend Dianne was coming up on Christmas Eve. I knew her presence would be our saving grace for the holidays. She would bring things she had baked, and insist we stop to smell the spices and drink fine beer. She would encourage Peter and Simon, the Scandinavian handlers, to tell stories about their homeland, where Christmas trees had candles balanced on their limbs.

I hooked up a team of my favorites first thing in the morning so I would be back in time for her arrival.

As soon as they saw the harnesses, the whole yard began barking and running around their houses. Who would be the lucky ones? Who would get to run first? They were all in such peak shape, their muscles rippling, and their movements a dance.

Oh, me, pick me! Let me go first!

I hooked up the brothers, Portland, Houston, and Bismarck and then the sisters Shasta, Tahoe, and Lassen. I put Reno in lead next to Salem, and we were off—galloping out of the dog yard leaving a powder trail of snow.

Jeff and Donna had built their home on the top of a wide ridge, at the edge of a lake where geese had once lived. Their driveway was a mile long, winding and climbing through the woods more in the manner of a trail than a roadway. It was one of three ways off the ridge to the network of trails where we trained the dogs—rarely the best choice with its steep inclines. The other trails wound tighter through the trees, but there the snow was often deeper, and there was more hope in slowing the teams down to a reasonable pace.

The first minutes with a fresh dog team are always insane. As soon as the dogs see the sled in position, they begin to work themselves into a primal frenzy, barking and testing the parameters of their chains. It is impossible to talk at these times. The chorus included every single dog in the yard, from the tiniest puppies to old Falcon reliving his past glories. Everybody wanted to go sledding.

Leaving the yard, I would bear down on the brake with every fiber of my own brute strength. I could never match theirs; from the starting point in the yard, it was downhill in all directions. It was like starting a roller-coaster ride at the edge of the initial plunge, with the prospect of the team's power and enthusiasm catapulting you into a helpless free fall. For me, the first minutes were always numbing with anticipation and fear, they did not last long, but their impressions ran deep into my dreams.

We crossed Goose Lake, then the small field beyond, and then up a slight hill into the woods. This was the time to reposition my hands, to make sure the team had their lines straight and clear to the towline. Once we entered the long chute that followed, for several anxious minutes there would be no chance to stop. It was fast and narrow, with solid little trees crowding the trail.

Salem stretched into his running gate, leading in complete ecstasy. Reno ran grinning beside him, his black-and-white coat shimmering as the first rays of sun bounced off the snow. These were my boys. This was my team. I laughed at my fears and they heard me and raced faster.

All along the trails we make decisions, as paths constantly branch off into different directions. Small loops have been added to the main trails— the chance to call commands and perfect them. Leaders are born, but leaders are also made, and we practiced every single run: gee here, haw there.

For some reason, on this beautiful morning of Christmas Eve I took a section of trail we never used when going away from the kennel. It was very steep and normally best at the end of a run, a last push uphill before dinner, a lesson that hard work was rewarded.

Salem had seen the turn and, wanting to please me, had leaped onto the trail before I could stop him. I had to admit it looked inviting, so smooth and trackless. It was nearly Christmas—why not celebrate with a break in routine?

The trail was lovely, the gentle curves perfect for the quick speed we were traveling. It was exciting; the kids were having so much fun. Tahoe was in prime form; her lope had the grace of a cougar. She stretched into every stride, oblivious to everything but the feel of her own body in flight. She was beautiful, and like a porpoise in the ocean or an eagle soaring, she made movement look magical.

We came around a corner, then the trail tilted, dropping away out of sight. The next moment paused, stretching before me in an interminable, sickening span. It gave me plenty of time to realize what a terrible, terrible mistake I had made. There was good reason why we only went up this section of trail, why we never—ever—went down.

Like a Sam Peckinpah film, everything happened in slow motion. The sled tipped forward, straight down the incline and instinctually I crouched to lower my body weight. We fell freely for a moment, and then the trail turned sharply to the right, taking the hill at a steep angle. Without a care in the world, the dogs made the ninety-degree turn.

My own leap to the uphill sled runner was a fraction too slow. The runners slid across a root that lay in the trail, exposed like a snake on a barren desert highway. The sled caught and tipped with the force of a startled rocket and I slammed into the tree going ten, maybe fifteen miles an hour. I heard the branches snap—the branches that ripped my grip free. I felt the weightlessness of the takeoff as the team launched themselves on down the trail.

But it is the smell that I remember most.

I could smell the sweet syrup of the spruce tree. I saw images of the real Christmas trees I insisted my parents buy. I thought of my college days in the pine forests of Montana, and Girl Scout camp in the Rockies.

I wondered if my neck was broken. The roar in my head confused me— was that surf? My body felt limp, totally relaxed in the cool snow, and I wondered if I could indeed hear the ocean. I lay perfectly still and before I opened my eyes, I wondered if one had been pierced, how it would be to wear a patch, if I would need to change colors to match what I wore—for the rest of my life. It was days, weeks, and yet, in the next moment I was up, and it was back to real time. Since I could move, I went tearing down the trail.

"Whoa boys! Whoa! Oh, please, whoa." In the distance, I saw the sled bouncing madly as the team crested the next hill. My wail seemed to hang suspended in the cold dense air.

"Oh, Salem—please, please, please. Whoa!"

I ran madly, waving my arms for momentum. By the time I climbed the top of the first hill, I knew it was stupid to chase them on foot. These were some of the finest sled dogs in the state, these were the rising stars, these were the result of generations of careful breeding, and these animals were born to run.

I turned toward the kennel, a good mile uphill through deep snow. At first I tried to run, but knew it was physically impossible. The air cut at my lungs, though an intense heat came from the rest of my body. I stripped off my coat and vest and dropped them in the trail. I went to take off my hat, and my hand met a sticky resistance. I could feel an odd bump on my forehead, but when my finger found what felt to be an opening, I quickly drew it away. I concentrated on marching and luckily, the air chilled the blood as it ran down my face, slowing it so I could feel it coming. I kept wiping my eyes, leaving red tracks on my gloves.

I felt disoriented, but I could walk, so I knew the injuries to my body were not as serious as the ones to my soul. My dear puppies were out there running by themselves. They could get hurt, and someone could die before I found them. Reno would lead them fast, too; Salem might try a new trail. Bismarck might fool around and tease Portland, pissing him off. Houston may miss a step and loop the tug around his leg and then falter, and then get dragged.

I cried as I ran, the tears and snot mixing with blood I could smell. The rhythm of my steps began to echo in my head like distant blows. Cold air sliced my lungs, forcing me to stop to let the spasms pass. I needed to catch my breath, and then go again for as long as possible. The hills stretched endlessly before me. Several times I wondered if I could do it, but knew I would twist every fiber of my soul trying. I had to get help. I had to get a snow machine. I had to find the team.

Simon was alone when I found him. Everyone else from the kennel was gone for the day. I burst into the kitchen yelling.

"Simon, you have to help me! I've lost my team! My team, my team, they're gone!"

He crossed the room and grabbed my shoulders. Cringing, he studied my forehead. In the warmth of the house, I could feel the blood melting and starting to ooze.

"Lisa. Are you all right?"

I pulled away from him; the cozy heat in the room panicked me further, feeling like a betrayal to the pups that were lost in the cold outside the door. I ran toward the door and, taking a deep breath, tried to steady my voice.

"I'm fine. But the dogs, we have to find the dogs. I'm taking a snow machine and heading toward Ravine Creek. Can you go toward Deneki Lakes? They could be anywhere!"

I hurried out the door before he could answer. I ran to a snow machine and began pulling and pulling the cord to start it. It just wouldn't fire, and kicking it in frustration, I ran to the other one.

This one roared to life, but I nearly ran off the trail less than a hundred yards from the kennel. Reality then hit me, and instinct from years of fishing on the sea took over. I needed to calm down. I had to stop the terrible images that were flooding my mind of tangled and injured dogs. I needed to think and drive this machine carefully. I needed to check the fuel and make a plan in my head. The frost on the gas cap burned my fingers as I twisted it open, but it was a relief to grip the seat with my knees as I launched out of the yard.

I raced the snow machine down the first trail I wanted to search, periodically swinging my glove across my face to clear the tears gelling on my eyelashes. My face burned from the cold, and childishly I hoped for frostbite. From where I had hit the tree, the team could have gone several directions. Each choice was a time commitment on my part. I stopped and tried to read the signs at crossroads, but there were hundreds of dog prints. We had been training a long time with no new snow. Moments were precious; someone could be choking as I idled along. I made a choice and headed toward Ravine Creek.

Eight dogs were gone. I imagined half my Iditarod team mangled, dead, or just missing forever. My dream of doing the Iditarod had turned into a nightmare and it was entirely my fault. For weeks, I had felt I was walking a thin line with Jeff. Though he rarely criticized, I couldn't help but imagine his thoughts as he saw me struggling to learn how to drive the sled. He was entrusting me with his next generation of team members, the precious result of years of careful planning, dogs who would assure him his place in history, and who would help pay for his children's college education.

I kept wrecking the sled, breaking it so many times, I had become crafty at lashing and bolting new pieces together. Often I came home from a training run with fragments of the trees that I had hit tangled in my hair, jammed into crevices of my sled bag. Snow would be unnaturally packed into my hood from being dragged headfirst along the trail. *How could Jeff allow these young dogs to travel with me through the Dalzell Gorge? How could he possibly have faith I could take them a thousand miles?*

I now remembered clearly the first time I had taken a team with Helge down the Ravine Creek Trail. The thrill of those first hills, the unbelievable magic of the white mountains around us and then the blue light of the early winter sunset. Jon Van Zyle had caught that color in the paintings he had done in the years following his own run in the Iditarod. I had imagined for a moment how it would feel to travel in that same light, for a thousand miles with a team of faithful friends, and it had seemed like such a wondrous and magical thing to do. Ravine Creek Trail had seemed so short that afternoon; before I knew it I had been back at my cabin, feeling as if I had stepped from a dream. Now three years later the trail seemed endless, and I desperately wished I were just in a bad dream; around each corner I chanted.

Oh, please, let them be there.

At the junction for the trail to the river, a whole new flood of terrible images came to mind. What if they took this way? What if they happily had taken this turn that led them to the Yanert River and all the perils it presented? Black holes in the ice, fast-moving overflow, and vicious traps set by men in search of furs—my babies were out there somewhere, and I just had to find them.

I followed the river a ways, but it extended for maybe thirty, forty miles in front of me. The wind coming down the river valley made my eyes water and burned my cheeks, but the possibilities here were infinite. I decided to somehow find a Bush plane if need be, to search the headwaters. First, I had to search nearer the kennel, along the other trails, perhaps even on the highway.

I drove and drove, finally returning to the kennel in need of gasoline. There I found Peter quietly putting away my harnesses and sled. He didn't stop working when I pulled into the yard. I spotted Lassen and then Tahoe at their houses. Quickly I swept my eyes over every doghouse until I was assured my team was all present. Everyone was back in their correct places, dozing peacefully in the late morning sunshine.

Peter seemed to avoid me, and in shame, I walked up to Salem. Standing silently, I stroked his back. His coat was ruffled, he seemed tired, but oddly he didn't look like someone who had recently avoided death. In fact, he looked . . . almost pleased.

I slinked away to my cabin. I could feel my forehead pounding with each heartbeat, and very slowly pulled the hat from my head. Blood caked my hair, and when I looked into a mirror, my stomach jumped. Like a tomato lost at the bottom of the grocery bag, half my forehead was swollen, red, and squishy. An ugly split ran several inches down to my eyebrow. It made me dizzy, and I quickly lay down on the carpet. It was Christmas Eve, and I couldn't imagine being more miserable.

After applying a compress of snow in a Ziploc baggie, I pulled my hat down low so the edge bumped my eyebrow, and reentered the dog yard. Peter told me the team had arrived back at the kennel in perfect form, lines tight like the pros. Not a single one came in tangled and not a single one missing a grin. His tone was flat and I read disappointment in every syllable. *How could I be so irresponsible?* Simon returned from his own search, and wanted to know about my head. I held my finger to my lips to silence him. It was nearly Christmas.

Jeff asked what had happened with the team, but then seeming indifferent, he simply walked away. I hadn't looked him in the eye, and I realized he thought I might cry and he didn't want to see. Actually, I had been more concerned with just keeping my uninjured side toward him as we spoke.

Dianne arrived with Terry, who had worked with me at Rohn. I swore them to secrecy before pulling off my hat. She hugged me and found ointments and aspirin. They unpacked my father's tree, and for dinner, Dianne helped me tie a scarf around my head, seductively low over one eye. I could see the hint of blue beginning where a black eye was on its way, but I dabbed on some foundation, put on a skirt and had no choice but to face Jeff.

He didn't notice. For once, I was glad he was so sad and preoccupied with missing his family. On Christmas Day, a neighbor invited us all for dinner. I felt ridiculous dressed like a gypsy and spent the day accepting countless compliments on my scarf. Whenever someone was close, Simon would say how pretty it was, just to see me squirm.

In the dog yard, I wore my hat low, avoiding everybody but especially Jeff. He mentioned I looked like Joe Redington's son, Raymie, who often wore his hat crooked, and I tried to make my laugh seem lighthearted. Days later, when Donna and the girls came home from New Zealand, I sat for hours in the living room—them in shorts showing off their tans, and me in my hat. I knew it was only a matter of time, but I also knew that every day healing would soften the shock.

After more than a week, it was almost a relief when my secret came out. Jeff, Cali, and I were driving three teams up on the Horse Trail when Jeff came back to trade one of the dogs out of my team. It was hot enough that I had pushed the hat up on my forehead, and I jumped when I heard his cry.

"What in the world happened to you!?"

CHAPTER 13

Ten Dogs, Ten Times

In January, I became fixated about improving my sled-driving abilities. The cuts on my face from Christmas healed, but I got another black eye. I broke another stanchion on the sled. I felt physically sick each time I approached certain trees on particular turns in the trails that surrounded the kennel. My sled runners knocked chunks off their trunks, but their branches scratched vicious like wildcats; feathers from my down parka fluttered from trees throughout the forest. Several times, I came close to hiking into the woods after dark with a chain saw.

"Ten dogs, ten times," Jeff would say. "If you can do the Horse Trail ten times with ten dogs, then you can do the Iditarod." There were parts of the Iditarod Trail that were more difficult, he said, but not by much. The goal seemed a concrete answer to my nightmares. It was like making a list and scratching through each accomplishment. There became a clear objective to my training trips.

The Horse Trail wound through the woods above Deneki Lakes and climbed a long ridge to the east of Carlo Mountain. It had everything for a perfect training trail: steep hills, tight turns, two ice crossings, and a section that required "side-hilling," which meant balancing on one runner on a slanting trail. There was even a place where the snow was frequently blown clear, exposing tall tussocks—mounds of grass frozen into stony pinnacles that could clip a wooden cross-member on the sled if you did not tilt it at the right moment. It was all good training for the dogs and great practice for me.

"Ten dogs, ten times" became my mantra. Though I sometimes noticed Jeff cringing at me, he never wanted specifics. When I asked for spare stanchions and brush bows to repair the sled, he never complained that I was quilting his equipment. Duct tape and old hockey sticks braced my poor sled for the battles I led it into. When I dryly told Morten that I always wore a hat to keep the pieces together when I wrecked, his eyes grew wide and immediately I regretted my confession. He couldn't seem to think of an appropriate response.

For a man known for his lack of communication, Jeff's kind words were small gifts to me. To the public, his communication skills were quite often black-and-white, hard and short. Yet with his family and a few close friends, he relaxed and, like the IRS, showed a kinder, gentler side. I now found myself desperate, and I treasured every subtle encouragement he offered. After years of hard work and long hours on the trail, we had become friends, and I knew he took his tutoring seriously. "Success is mandatory" was his personal mantra, and he said it often, just so I could hear.

For weeks I drove just eight dogs. Their power seemed to keep my sled just on edge—sixteen was a number I couldn't even imagine. Of course, I could take larger teams on the other trails, the straighter, wider ones, but the Horse Trail wound tightly through the woods, and there was very little snow to bank the curves or cover the rocks.

I eased my way up to nine dogs by adding a little girl to the team. That night success had me privately celebrating in my cabin. The next day I flipped the sled, though high on a ridge where you had to side-hill—the technique of balancing on the thin aluminum track. When I tried to jerk the sled up, I missed a beat and the back-swing tipped the sled over, downhill on the incline. I did not let go, but I went back to eight dogs, and still hit two trees.

The shame and embarrassment ate away at my self-confidence. I felt I could do nothing right anymore. I put gasoline in the diesel truck; I forgot to add chicken to the dog food; I didn't pay my Blue Cross on time; I even burned everything I tried to cook. There were nights when I was crying myself to sleep.

Jeff kept methodically coaching me. Sometimes it felt like Mushing 101. He showed me how to put my foot out alongside the sled runner so it acted as a ski. This added tremendous stability on the turns and I was amazed that I hadn't learned it in the previous years. The first year, though, I had hardly stepped on a sled, and the second year there hadn't been much snow, so I had spent most of the time on the gee-pole sled. I was also forty-two and had never been described as graceful. I tried to convince myself I was wrecking, not because I was stupid, but because I was just plain clumsy.

Friends of the Kings, who were mushers themselves, came for a visit, and I made some runs with them. Suspiciously, after every trip, they casually pointed out ways I could have driven the sled better, politely giving me helpful hints. I knew how the unsolicited advice had come about, but it did not hurt my feelings that my driving abilities had become a public issue. I may have been embarrassed, but more than anything, I just felt desperate.

Then I did the Horse Trail with nine dogs, and then one day, finally, ten. Ellen and Jeff toasted my success at dinner, but I was too afraid to celebrate. The next day I again had ten dogs, and though I did dump the sled, the recovery had been so perfect; secretly I felt it should count.

I entered the Tustumena 200 race on the Kenai Peninsula to gain some experience and confidence. David was helping, and I laughed watching him deal with the dogs. If someone was starting to fight, he quickly ran over to them and bared his own teeth, growling. I had never actually seen anyone else use this technique, but it seemed to work and I didn't want to discourage his enthusiasm. I did have to turn my head, though, so he wouldn't see the teeth of my own smiles.

David, handling for both Jeff and me, was nervous. Twenty-four dogs seemed like a lot to him. Typical of his work ethic, he took this job in a no-nonsense manner, and I really appreciated both his just being there and his meticulous help. I knew that growing up in California, he had never dreamed he would someday be dealing with a team of barking, lunging huskies. It was obviously not his thing. It did not come easily, but he did it for me, and I was grateful for his support. Living apart for these past winters had been especially difficult for him, and I felt a tinge of guilt. While he had lived at home alone, I had been out on the adventures.

Because we had spent so much of our lives together, I was surprised when he did not immediately know the names of all my puppies.

"That's not Salem, David! That's Potter! And Lassen is the one who runs just like Jenna!"

I tried quickly to fill him in on why each dog was quite unique—how these guys came from the superstar Kanga. And, of course, the mother of those girls was Jenna.

"I like Jenna," he said. Not that he didn't like the other dogs, but eighty were too many to get to know. It bothered him that there was not time to bring each and every one into my cabin at night. He picked out Jenna from the barking lot and, without knowing Jenna's status as an Iditarod superstar, he had pointed to her regal pose while all around the dogs were racing around their houses.

"I like that one. Who is that?" he had asked on the very first visit to the kennel.

The start of the Tustumena was wild. Tahoe had watched the crowds with a slightly worried look, but walked to the towline with grace and dignity. She waited patiently, nervously shifting her weight from paw to paw. Once his harness was on, Salem forgot people were watching and had eyes only for me, and some distant point ahead past the crowds, down the trail. Lassen crouched as I approached with the harness, ready to spring like a cat. Then she was barking at everyone, nose skyward in delight. She rammed Shasta with her shoulder and appeared to laugh.

Fun! Like, look at us! We are Race Dogs!

The Caribou Hill trails were known as a roller coaster of steep climbs and sharp drops, and because the path was wide, I was not afraid of flipping the sled. My team worked hard and rested well, but after the mandatory six-hour rest at the halfway point, they were raring to go.

Another musher named Vern Halter was due to leave at the same time, and since I knew his reputation as an excellent dog driver, I decided he would be a good example to tail. We would follow him out of the checkpoint, across the road, and back into the woods. I moved my team up behind his in the starting chute and waited for the countdown. At the correct time, I pulled my snow hook in hot pursuit.

Vern's team easily crossed the road, taking the trail that ran parallel with the highway. My guys were thrilled with being back in motion after a good long rest, happy to be sled dogs in this sled-dog race. They charged out of the checkpoint and bounded toward the road crossing. In a single, frozen moment I saw the leaders thinking, and then the combined leap with their collective "good idea": *Why take that little trail?*

We could see Vern's team cruising on the route that followed a gully that ran parallel to the road. *Why,* thought the puppies, *why not take this first nice asphalt trail right here? It's so beautiful and wide!* As a single unit, the little darlings shot past the poor volunteer holding his "Stop" sign. I hardly had time to shout "Whoa" as we leapt onto the Sterling Highway.

Onto a highway, and we were indeed in motion, and there was nothing I could do to slow the team. Quick math made me realize how serious things were—us going fifteen miles an hour meeting an oncoming car doing forty. It was a terrifying realization. I knew from my other experience in Denali Park that it was useless ruining the brake on the asphalt, and though I steadily called "Whoa," I desperately tried to come up with a plan.

I was strangely calm, as if I was watching the scene from a distance. I noted wryly that the centerline of the highway indicated we were in a no-passing zone, and I had to smile. Soon we passed Vern, who was below us in the trail that still ran parallel to the highway. Later he shook his head laughing.

"Your team looked really great! Man, they looked like they were having fun!"

And they were. I was the one with full-color images of flattened skunks and cats tainting my mood. Using my weight, I tried to work the sled closer to the edge of the road. Progress came in inches. I looked down at the shoulder of the highway speeding by and realized what I had to do. I pulled my hat down lower and squeezed the handle bow tighter. I counted to ten, looked down once more, and then counted all over again. I checked ahead of me for a miracle, but saw none. Before I reached nine—for the third time—I hurled my body sideways, flipping the sled on its side.

With age comes a number of wisdoms. Undoubtedly, the benefits often outweigh the problems. I knew I had to jump, and I accepted this calmly. Right before my shoulder hit the snow I cringed, thinking about the deductible on my health insurance. Luckily, blessedly though, the snow was deep and the extra resistance slowed the team immediately to a halt. Everyone was panting, looking back at me, seeming pretty pleased with themselves. I tried to hide my own smile from them. We had gone really, really fast.

There is a huge difference between running a puppy team and a team of adults. With a puppy team after the initial excitement wore off, they slept hard at the checkpoints. They gobbled their snacks, but refused to eat real meals. I stopped them often, petting everyone and wrestling with Bismarck. He was one happy guy.

Bismarck was an exact replica of his dad, Yuksi, at the same age. Brian, the man who had raised the famous sire, had told me this with awe. He was such a beautiful dog, long legged, with a coat the color of polished walnut. Watching Bismarck move was like seeing the young thoroughbreds in Kentucky darting behind the white plank fences. Even if you didn't love the animals, you couldn't help but appreciate the beauty and grace of the creature.

He loved to play, and even when he was tired, he would still try to paw me as his eyes slowly closed. A hundred and seventy miles with lots of hills, by the time we reached the last checkpoint I knew I wanted to let the dogs nap. We weren't last, but pretty darn close. I just wanted to finish the race with happy dogs; I wanted it to be fun for them.

The Four Corners checkpoint was a cement-block building in the middle of nowhere. It sat high on a hill where four wide trails met and was basically used as emergency shelter for the local snow machine club. The volunteers working the race were a rowdy group of what appeared to be senior citizens. They made me feel so welcomed that I hurried inside to visit while the dogs slept. They insisted on making me hot cider and dished up a bowl of stew, picking out extra meat to add to my serving. I felt loved and sleepy in the cozy cabin, and would have dozed, but was having such a good time I didn't want to miss anything. Everyone was chattering, telling jokes and stories. Someone asked about my team and I murmured.

"None of my dogs are even a year and a half old." I let my eyes close. "Both their moms—Kanga and Jenna—and the dad, Yuksi, have run the Iditarod several times." Then almost to myself I added, "There is something about Yuksi that is very sensual."

I was starting to nod off, so the last word came out long and luxuriously. "S-e-n-s-u-a-l."

The room went completely silent. The sudden quiet surprised me, and I opened my eyes. Every single person in the room was staring at me, and they looked confused. Had I done something? Had I snored or worse, something else? Could it have been my choice of words? Sensual? Several of my newfound friends even looked . . . worried.

Slowly, I realized that what I said next was very important. I was tired, but not oblivious. I could leave the checkpoint feeling like a pampered grandchild or I could leave feeling terribly misunderstood. I looked for the kindest face in the crowd, a woman who reminded me of my mamaw. Using my most angelic voice I explained, "When you pet him, he growls, real low like a purr. His eyes get dreamy. If you run your hand down his body, he arches his back and leans into you. He acts just like a cat." The room seemed to expel a communal sigh of relief.

"His kids are just like him—sensitive," I said. I was relieved to hear someone giggle, then everybody else join in. The room went back to its bustling self.

I finished the race third from last. It was not a star performance, but I certainly learned a lot about the dogs and myself. Back at the kennel, while the race dogs rested, I immediately took ten of my puppies up to the Horse Trail, and made the loop without wrecking. I was tired, but giddy by the time I reached home. There were just enough hours left of daylight to do one more trip. I hooked up another team of ten dogs, and returned to the dog yard just as the sun was setting—my teeth chilling dry from grinning.

The next day Jeff came on a run with me. We both had teams of his powerful adult race dogs. A hundred yards from the finish of the windy trail, I clipped a tree hard enough to be jerked from the sled. My face plowed into the dirty snow, and for a split second I contemplated not getting up. Jeff caught the team, and I knew I had nowhere to hide. We didn't look at each other when I retrieved them. It would have been my fourth straight success, but now I had to start totally over. Ten dogs, ten times, maybe it was impossible. Maybe, for me, doing the Iditarod was impossible.

I finished my dog-yard chores and walked past Tahoe and Reno, who twirled on their chains waiting to be unhooked to join me for the night. I went to my cabin, and before I took off my boots, I turned off the light. For a while, I sat on the couch fully dressed, but finally crawled into bed for the sake of the covers. I went to bed without dinner, not that I was punishing myself. I was just too depressed to stay sitting upright any longer than life required. Later the phone rang, but I didn't answer it. I dreamed, or it may have been real—that someone knocked on the door—but I couldn't turn my face from the wall. The night was endless, and morning came too soon. Another day was about all I could bear.

Jeff came into the feed room, and with fervent enthusiasm told me about his new idea. It sounded like a boot-camp drill and was hard to imagine, but I tried to put some spirit into my agreement.

"You need to be able to pull yourself back up onto the sled going down the trail, so we'll simulate you falling off. I'll be on a team in front, so if you lose your grip, I can grab the dogs."

It sounded fine, until out on the trail the first time when he yelled "Down!" We were going at least ten miles an hour down a straight stretch of the trail and by the time I got the nerve up to ease myself off the sled— it was too late. We had come to some curves and I had to wait. A moment later, he again yelled "Down!"

This time, gripping tightly to the wooden stanchions, I eased my feet, then my legs, and finally my hips, off the sled runners until I was lying totally prone in the snow, whizzing along at an astounding speed, suspended by my two little arms.

Of course, I had been in this position before, just never voluntarily. Usually I somewhat panicked, fearing that if I moved or loosened my grip, that I would lose the team. Now I gritted my teeth, twisting and pulling myself back up onto the sled. I had to climb and then balance on one runner before shifting upward. Somehow it worked. Jeff gave me a thumbs-up signal, but not believing in resting on one's laurels, moments later, I heard him yell again.

"Down!"

The point was to build not only the muscles needed to pull myself back up onto the sled runners, but even more importantly, build the confidence to believe I could do it. Upper-body strength is very helpful in dog mushing. I had whined about not having enough to my coach, but he was unsympathetic.

"It is technique over brawn," he said repeatedly. "Absolutely."

And so I practiced my techniques. I skied along using my boot on every turn. I stayed in constant motion on the sled runners, adjusting my balance to every nuance in the trail. I balanced on one runner when the trail ran on the slightest angle, and I practiced jumping off and running beside the sled on tight turns. I had studied this move on nearly every video I had seen on the Iditarod—it looked so dramatic—but I had always been too frightened to try it myself.

One morning, trying to sound lighthearted, I asked Virgil to drag my sled behind the snow machine as I skied with both boots going down the driveway. The blue clouds of exhaust nearly choked me, but I lived for the encouragement in his face.

"You did real good, Lisa! You're getting it down now!" Virgil looked so proud, so happy with my success, as if I were his daughter taking her first steps. I had to turn away before he saw the tears. I was still feeling so ashamed, so unworthy.

CHAPTER 14

Still Just a Little Girl

*R*evolving stacks of lists were my crutch during the last half of February. Using paper to put order to the chaos in my mind helped ease some of my fears. It allowed me to present a calm façade to those around me. Yellow notepads covered every subject I could think of: what exactly was going into the sled, what was to be packed into the dog truck for the trip to Anchorage, what sixteen dogs would eat every few hours, what bills, like Blue Cross, that I had to pay before leaving. I even listed what my mother could do for fun in Anchorage if she became bored with the Iditarod. Shyly I made a list of things David should take to Nome for me—in case I made it.

I kept practicing on the Horse Trail, but eventually it became too late to keep count. Some days I was successful; others, I was not. One foot went in front of the other. I tried on the exact outfit I would be wearing for the entire race, and packed my sled with everything I would be carrying. I hooked up a sixteen-dog towline, but only put ten dogs in harness. This way I was able to experience driving something that, bow to stern, reached nearly forty feet.

Cabela's, an outdoor gear retail business, was one of my main race supporters. They supplied me with a variety of arctic gear and paid my entry fee. As one of the major sponsors of the Iditarod, they also kept a Web site specifically following the race. It was an excellent resource for people around the world interested in the Iditarod. With a wealth of background knowledge, Joe Runyan, the race champion of 1989, wove history and sled-dog trivia into reports he made of current race happenings.

"Rookie of the Year" in its true Iditarod form was an award given at the end of the race to the top-placing rookie of that year. Doug Swingley, the current champion, had once won it, as did Ramy Brooks and Jason Barron. In 2002, Cabela's hosted a Rookie of the Year on their Web site—but it was strictly a popularity contest. Viewers could place votes on their favorite new musher, and a running tab could be viewed during the last couple of weeks before the Iditarod.

I was busy with my lists, and rarely got on the computer at all. Late one night I clicked onto the site and found my name near the top of the list. People were actually voting for me! I knew it was silly, but I felt a blush of pride; out of forty-five rookies, my name was in the top ten.

A few days later, I reached the top-five position, and one night I was, at least for a while, the most popular rookie running in the 2002 Iditarod! I was too embarrassed to mention it to anyone at the kennel, but for several days, it gave me a good reason to laugh, and I checked the site each night before going to bed.

One evening, my brother Glenn called from Dutch Harbor. He fished for crab in the hazardous waters off the Aleutian Chain that extended west from mainland Alaska. He was not going to make it to Anchorage for my send-off, and I cherished the rare telephone calls he made while in port. Only to him could I confess.

"Jeez, Glenn, this is wild. There is this rookie contest and people are voting for me. I mean, lots of people! I was number one for a while, though now I think I'm in third place. The two Norwegian guys, Sørlie and Backen, are ahead of me now, but it keeps going back and forth. I don't even know that many people with computers!"

There was a long pause and then I heard him giggle—a thousand miles away. It was loud and clear.

"What?" I said, sensing something.

"We-l-l-l, little sis . . . " I am actually older than he, except when he feels guilty.

"What's up, Glenn?" His giggle had a devilish tone, and I could sense the presence of the fake halo. I had seen it thousands of times growing up.

"Ummm, Dad has been voting for you," he said, and there was a long, revealing pause. "A lot."

Suddenly it dawned on me why the numbers of votes cast were possibly so radically different. Most of the mushers had fewer than a hundred, many fewer than even fifty votes. The Norwegians and I were quickly accumulating hundreds, and now in the week before the race, thousands of votes. It had vaguely puzzled me, but I had been too pre-occupied to dwell on the differences. My father, of course. My father.

"Dad has gone nuts. The Web site put on cookies or something, so he couldn't just vote at home; he had to go to the Russellville library and use the public computers there as well. He does it all day, every day. He sits at one computer then waits in line for another. He puts in votes—full time— so you'll win the Cabela's Rookie of the Year contest."

A hot flash rolled over me and holding the phone to my ear, I carefully laid down on the couch.

"You're kidding."

I imagined the inevitable meeting of Cabela's bigwigs in Anchorage before the race start. How would I ever face them? Their site received over a million hits during the weeks surrounding the Iditarod. This was big business.

"Well, you're kind of popular out here, too," Glenn giggled. "I have the whole fleet, whenever we come into port to deliver fish, they vote for you, too."

I was horrified and felt the familiar burn in my stomach growing hotter. I wanted to throw up. I wanted to cry, and yet deep down realized I was also a little tickled. After hanging up from my brother I found myself sitting on the couch, laughing hysterically through a flood of tears. My father loved me! Damn this ridiculous event!

Before calling down to Kentucky, though, I once again logged onto the Cabela site. I now had close to four thousand votes. Only the Norwegians came anywhere close.

"Dad, we need to talk." I tried to keep my voice lighthearted. My father was so far away from me now and wouldn't be able to come up to see me take off. He was missing a very big event in my life. I had to be sensitive, but I knew I couldn't pussyfoot around. Before I could lose my nerve, I blurted out, "Dad, you have to stop voting for me."

It was as if he had been waiting for his secret to be found out—and with a hand on my forehead, feeling the oncoming fever, I smiled at the flood of words coming over the line.

"Those Norwegians! I think they're cheating, I don't know how they do it. You can't click the mouse that much! It must be automated! You were ahead yesterday, but this morning . . . "

"Dad!"

"The librarian here can't figure me out, never seen me before and now I live down there. I go to Wal-Mart for lunch and then I am back at it. Sunday is tough. After church I drive over to Bowling Green. They have a bigger library, longer hours. These Norwegians are nuts!"

I covered the phone so he couldn't hear my laughter. He was just doing his part. My mother was coming up, but my father was right there with me as well. I cherished this funny offering, this strange gift to me in my hour of need. I used it during the next weeks—to make me smile when I thought that running the Iditarod was going to be the biggest mistake of my life.

More friends started calling, and though I usually was not in the cabin to talk to them, I clung to their kind words of encouragement captured on the recorder. Finally, or all too soon, it was time to pack up the truck and head south.

Jeff and I left the kennel early Wednesday morning with my team. The plan was for us to set up the dog-parking area at the hotel in downtown Anchorage. The rest of the crew was coming the next day with his team. It was more important that his dogs rest as long as possible, in their own beds, before entering the crowded madness of the next few days.

David was flying in from Kodiak and meeting us in Anchorage. Bad weather frequently delayed flights off the island, and I was silently praying for clear skies. Both of our mothers were flying in, and I was desperate for

David to ease some of the heavy burden off my shoulders. I wanted to go home and cry, to have this whole nightmare already over. Jeff and I were hardly speaking. He had run out of words to comfort me, and I was speechless in my fears. We both knew the only answer was to get on the trail as soon as possible—and let Fate begin her choosing.

When we arrived at the hotel's parking lot, we set out chains, attaching my team in the most remote corner. Jeff drove off on errands, leaving me alone with my powerful athletes in the center of the city. They were wound up after the long drive, and I wished I could take them on a quick run to calm us all down. They had never been in a city before, and the excitement was almost too much, threatening to pull out the picket as they lunged in circles, barking madly.

I cringed to see the lights of a fire engine approaching, but ended up laughing as it sped by the hotel. Instead of being frightened by the siren, the puppies instantly stopped their barking and pointed their noses straight up. They howled into the city skies—their muscled little bodies lined up like battery-operated toys, squeezing the notes out past the high-rises. For a moment, all my fears disappeared. I was consumed with love of them, and this place where the ancient call of sled dogs can echo down city streets.

David's flight made it on time, and the Moms arrived to do some much-needed mothering. Dena organized the kitchenette in the hotel room and spoke in whispers. Holding my mom's arm, she took her to the parking lot to visit the dogs. Mom giggled with the puppies and quickly picked her favorites. At first, she was afraid of Hardtack, whose rugged good looks reminded her of the wolves on the Discovery Channel; though soon she fell in love with his beautiful almond eyes and the way he closed them when his ears were caressed.

She seemed to be enjoying herself, except when I mentioned anything about the race. Then she would bite her lip and go silent. She desperately looked at David, and even Dena (who at least had been to Nome before), but they could offer very little comfort. I was forty-two years old, but still her little girl, and it was such a long way to travel alone in the cold.

Shyly she handed me a laminated little booklet she had made in Kentucky. She had found Don Bowers's "Trail Notes" on the Iditarod Web site and copied them with a tiny map of the state of Alaska. A thin black line showed the way. Before handing it to me, I saw her suck in her breath to steady her voice.

"I don't want you getting lost," she said trying to smile.

Later, coming out of the bedroom, she caught me in my long underwear and cried out. My legs were long sticks under the light fabric, my arms angled and boney. I knew it had gotten pretty bad in the last weeks, but there had been no emotional energy to fight it. I had given up on my battle with eating. Instead of looking like a healthy athlete ready to race, my body was something you turned away from in shock.

"Lisa. You have to eat," she said over and over, bribing me with food she carried now in her pockets.

"Mom, I can't!" I finally snapped, and guilt made my stomach burn.

Seeing my reflection in the full-length hotel mirror frightened me as well. Not only did my body look like someone else's, it did not look strong enough to carry me a thousand miles. The expression on my face, which had become fixed over the past weeks, was not a pleasant sight either for my poor friends and family. The angle of my cheekbones was too sharp, and it mirrored the grim position of my jaw. There was such a deep darkness under my eyes.

I wanted to tell everyone how sorry I was to put them through this, but was too afraid to speak of such things. My nightmares were burning the life out of me, but I couldn't describe them out loud to anyone—I was afraid I might not be able to pull myself back out of the fetal position I knew would follow.

All of the mushers were required to attend an all-day meeting two days before the race, and I sought out other rookies. Karen Land was from Indiana, basketball country. I felt a special kinship with her. She was as thin and pale as I was, but had lost the confident sparkle that had drawn me to her at the rookie meeting in December. I still had hopes we could travel part of the trail together, and we both agreed that once we got out of town, we would start eating again.

To raise funds, the Iditarod Trail Committee auctions rides with the mushers for the first miles out of Anchorage. Of course, I had worried about wrecking the sled with my "Idita-Rider" in downtown Anchorage, but after meeting her, I knew she could handle anything. For Susie, I had to pretend to be happy and excited; for the entire introductory luncheon, I acted as if I was delighted and confident about the entire adventure. I told stories, teasing her about my tendency to run the sled into trees and anything in the way. For a whole hour I pretended what I so truly wanted to believe—that everything was going to be all right.

Changes and conditions of the trail were carefully discussed at the meeting. I was thrilled to hear the snow was deep, better than it had been in years. Every year at this same meeting, there is a traditional toast of champagne and a group photo taken of the mushers. I could hardly look around as I stood among the familiar faces of these racers I had known for years. Briefly, though, I allowed myself to be excited. Martin Buser was standing behind me and Linda Plettner was at my side. Doug Swingley, the reigning champion, was in the back row. For the first time I was with these people, not as a volunteer helping them on the race, but with my own team of dogs, my own race agenda. It still stunned me that I would soon be an Iditarod musher.

▲ Every board for our house was brought out on an eight-hour boat ride and then pulled up the cliff with pulleys. We make our own electricity with solar panels and a small hydroelectric system. The local population is twelve—when everyone is present! We are more like family than neighbors. SALLY RITTENHOUSE PHOTO

▲ Blessed with a string of "paradises" in my life—I have spent two decades fishing from beaches on the west side of Kodiak Island. My fish camp is called—Paradise. LISA FREDERIC PHOTO

▼ I grew up hating the salmon patties my mom made in Kentucky—and yet now after commercially fishing for Alaskan salmon for nearly twenty-five years I think eating it is one of life's greatest pleasures. MAUREEN REGAN PHOTO

► My first year as a volunteer on the Iditarod Trail had me working in the coastal village of Shaktoolik. It's a village famous for its winds (Libby Riddles left out of here in a blizzard securing her first-place win) but it is also a village known for its children. Don-don was one of my favorites.
LISA FREDERIC PHOTO

▼ Running the Junior Iditarod has been a goal for each of Jeff and Donna King's daughters. Cali was the first girl ever to win and here Tessa proudly wears her race bib. Ellen had her racing debut in 2006. JEFF AND DONNA KING PHOTO

▲ Jeff told me if I could do the Horse Trail ten times with ten dogs in harness, I could do the Iditarod. It became my mantra. The views were spectacular, but I routinely lost control of the sled on sections of the trail, slamming into trees and coming home with new bruises almost daily. MORTEN FONSECA PHOTO

▲ As the winter progressed it became more and more embarrassing to face anyone. Nerves kept me from eating and I weighed less than I did in high school. I wrecked the sled so often I nearly always had a black eye or lacerations on my face. LISA FREDERIC PHOTO

▶ Coming into Elim I was all smiles— just under 100 miles to go! Little did I know how a blizzard would slow me down. JASPER BOND PHOTO

▲ We spent weeks preparing the drop bags, which were then hauled out to the different checkpoints by the Iditarod Air Force. They were filled with booties, ointments for the dogs' feet, kibble, a variety of meats—as well as things I needed—spare sled parts, changes of clothing, batteries, snacks, and meals. I sent out lots of spare socks, but only changed them twice the whole trip! VIRGIL TROUT PHOTO

▼ David stood with me on the runners to slow down the team as we made our way down Fourth Avenue in downtown Anchorage. My Idita-Rider, Susie, had been warned of my tendency to wreck, but she was too thrilled to care. MARILYN WHYTE PHOTO

▲ Salem—the coolest dog of all time. LISA FREDERIC PHOTO

▼ The kids in the village of Takotna were let out of school to help at the checkpoint. They parked teams, hauled water, and kept warm fires going. They adored the dogs and Lassen especially enjoyed all the attention. LISA FREDERIC PHOTO

▲ Martin Buser, the new champion in 2002, met every musher who came in under the burled arch. After congratulating those of us in the back of the pack though, he quickly stepped out of the limelight.
LISA FREDERIC PHOTO

◄ David looked worse than I did by the end of the race. He was as worried about me breaking my neck or getting lost as he was of living with me if I didn't make it!
MARILYN WHYTE PHOTO

▼ Not exactly Bluegrass Country, my mom borrowed long underwear and came to Alaska for my Iditarod to cheer me on. MARILYN WHYTE PHOTO

▲ Hardtack has the almond-shaped eyes of a Walt Disney wolf—and a personality to match. LISA FREDERIC PHOTO

▼ In May of 2000 Jenna had a litter of pups. Lassen (center) and Tahoe (right) grew up to be not only incredible sled dogs, but some of my very best friends. Both were stars on my team, as well as Jeff's. JEFF AND DONNA KING PHOTO

▲ Bismarck—the George Clooney of the sled-dog world! So handsome, so debonair—always looking around! LISA FREDERIC PHOTO

▼ (Left) Utah's delicate size belied her huge desire to pull. LISA FREDERIC PHOTO

▼ (Right) Tahoe spent every night in my cabin, watching me with the same regal eyes as her famous mother, Jenna. Whenever either of them was around I always sat up straighter. LISA FREDERIC PHOTO

CHAPTER 15

Finally—the Iditarod Start

Saturday morning we had the dogs loaded into the trailer by seven o'clock and drove the short distance to Fourth Avenue in silence. I realized the grim faces of my family mirrored my own and took a deep breath.

"We aren't going to a funeral, you guys!"

The street and several adjoining blocks were already noisy with dog teams and diesel trucks. While the sled and dogs were unloaded, I paced around my gear. David rechecked every millimeter of my sled, every zipper and every knot. Though he actually had spent very little time mushing, he knew what the weakest links were, and carefully made sure every detail was in perfect order. Friends and strangers streamed by to meet the dogs. I introduced Bismarck because he was so handsome, and Utah because she was so delightfully petite. Andy Moderow stopped at the truck and assured me this would be one of the most fun days of my Iditarod. He had run a team for Martin Buser in 2001 and been unofficially voted the cheeriest rookie of all time.

"Enjoy every moment of it!" he said.

Susie came by with her husband, and I showed her where she would sit in the sled and warned her again to hang on extra tight. Everyone laughed, and I had to admit, it was fun. The noise level was steadily growing as the crowds grew and the dogs became more excited, but everyone seemed to be having a great time.

Volunteers were everywhere keeping order to the chaos, and finally one came calmly to tell us we had just minutes until departure. Suddenly we were in a flurry to get booties on my team, to get the mothers on their way to the official starting chute. I felt so grateful for the dedication of my friends who focused like professionals, though the noise and excitement was nearly overwhelming. With a kiss to her husband, Susie climbed into the sled, and we began making our way to the starting line.

David and I both rode the brake of the sled while the dogs were led through the crowds. At the prerace banquet I had drawn starting number forty-four, but even though nearly half the teams had already left, the noise in downtown was still tremendous. I had Alto and Utah in lead because they were the most experienced in the team and (I was hoping) could handle the pressure.

Teams leave at two-minute intervals, so we worked our way down the street behind other mushers. I vaguely remembered watching this scene as a university student during one of my first years in Alaska nearly twenty years earlier. It had all seemed so noisy and foreign to me.

Some of my dearest friends from the Iditarod helped hold my sled as we waited for the final countdown. It was impossible to fathom that just a few years ago, these people were all strangers, and the world of sled dogs was a complete unknown. I desperately looked into the crowd for my mother's face, but couldn't find her. David gave me a hug, and then stepped away. A friend bent close to whisper words of encouragement in my ear—then the numbers ran out and I was off.

" . . . she's on her way to Nome!"

The departure from downtown Anchorage on Saturday is strictly a ceremonial start for the Iditarod. It is an opportunity for fans to meet the mushers and see the dog teams up close. The real competition actually begins on Sunday, with a restart just north of the city where trails lead directly into the wilderness. Today hundreds of people lined the streets, and I was surprised to find myself smiling and waving. I had never once imagined the glamour in this part of the Iditarod.

The dogs seemed oblivious to the details of the city. After leaving the streets, the trail followed the bike paths that Anchorage turns into ski trails in the winter. I was so happy that my passenger got a taste of this part of mushing. For a while, the only sounds were the runners on the snow and the excited tiny yelps from the dogs. I briefly put my hand on her shoulder, but we didn't speak. This was the real magic and why we were both here.

People dressed in heavy winter outfits lined many parts of the trail. I could see them holding the current newspaper, which had printed the name and picture of all the mushers running in the race this year. When they could make out my bib number, I could see them scramble to find me on the list.

"All the way to Nome, Lisa!"

"Go girl!"

"You can do it, Lisa!"

I hadn't expected people to call out my name. I hadn't known that complete strangers would go to the trouble to read about and cheer on a rookie. Around each turn in the trail, a new group stood poised to encourage us. I was shocked to see even handmade signs.

"Rookies need love, too!"

"Yea, Kodiak!"

"Eat salmon!" I laughed when I saw this one. The woman had done her homework.

These people did not know me, and yet they seemed to care that I was trying to do this silly thing. I was dumbfounded. I wanted to thank them in a manner that really showed my appreciation, but the team was barreling down the trail. The faces flew by. Often I would look over my shoulder to wave yet another time, but then ahead I would hear more cheers and new voices. I laughed with real joy. This was Alaska. This was the magic of the race I had forgotten in the months of training.

David and the Moms met us after the short ceremonial ride, and we drove back to the hotel to spend one last night together. Sunday afternoon I would finally leave the road system and begin winding through the eleven hundred miles that crossed the state. I wouldn't see any more of my family until I made it to Nome . . . if I made it to Nome. Once again, David and I went over my gear in the parking lot; we cuddled and played with the dogs. *Who among them would be my stars? Would any fail? Would one of these young dogs save my life?*

Potter and Latte wouldn't stop barking. Lassen was obsessed with teasing whomever I put her near, and Shuman bit Reno. Tahoe paced and watched the traffic with a worried expression. Bismarck swung his hips and smiled at anyone who looked his way. He was certainly happy and loved it most when children stopped by and ran their hands down his back. Whenever I went back to the room, Salem stared at the door of the hotel, always the first to spot me through the glass doors when I returned.

I wanted to ease my family's worries by appearing lighthearted myself, but once again, I was scared sick. The dogs were screaming to go— anywhere—and this time I would have all sixteen hooked up together. I still could not imagine driving so many at one time in their current mental condition. The dogs were used to running, and after being cooped up for so many days, they were beginning to turn into manic strangers. Every move they made was a blind lunge. Their frenetic barking chilled me.

Early Sunday morning we drove the hour north to Wasilla. A field had been turned into a parking lot for the restart. Hundreds of dogs were barking as mushers and handlers scrambled to get ready. Being a past champion, fans constantly surrounded Jeff's truck, but this time I was not part of his pit crew. I was jealous of how happy and carefree his handlers were—and shamefully wished I were just a worker as well.

Oh, to be free from this huge weight on my chest.

Jeff came over to wish me well, but we had little to say. By the time we saw each other again my fate would be sealed—all my work and his mentoring would be answered. Not only was I taking his dogs, I was also taking all his extra effort and the personal time he took to prepare me for this adventure. I still felt like such a remedial sled driver and now, for the first time, faced hooking up all sixteen dogs into one long and powerful team. I felt totally inadequate. But I knew Jeff hated a sniveler, so I kept my jaw tight to keep him from seeing it tremble. He had few words for me, and I could tell, in his mind, he was already on the trail, running his own race. The umbilical cord had been severed.

"Take good care of those dogs, and go fast like the wind," I said bravely. Taking a deep breath, I lowered my voice to appear confident. "I'll see you in Nome."

David and I avoided anything but the briefest eye contact. We both knew that with him, I could allow myself to break down completely, and this was not the time. The stakes in this adventure were high for him. Emotionally transparent, I would not be pleasant company if some disaster kept me from making it to Nome. He must have been as worried about life with me if I failed, as he was of me killing myself in the Dalzell Gorge.

It was a huge relief to hear the final countdown—to finally be starting the Iditarod for real, rather than just worrying about it. With sixteen dogs we flew away from the banners and through the birch forests of Knik with so much power there was literally no way I could stop them. I clung to the handle bow and desperately hoped nothing went wrong until they were tired enough that I could stop the sled.

Watching them as we sped along, though, I was surprised to realize, yes they were an uncontrollable force as a group, but individually they were still some of my best friends. I knew each one so well—had slept and eaten and breathed the smell of their bodies for two years. Perhaps going with them, and attempting the Iditarod, was not such a terrible mistake after all.

CHAPTER 16

The Ring of Warnings

*I*n January I had raced in the Knik 200, which had followed these first few miles to Yentna Station. I'd only had twelve dogs, but now with four more, I felt like I had put another motor on my skiff. The sled hurled through the birch trees like a missile, and my hands cramped from squeezing the handle bow.

After a couple of hours, we crossed Flat Horn Lake and I started seeing mushers parked in the trees. We had traveled more than forty miles, and I knew I should stop because the afternoon was getting warm, but I kept rejecting each good spot I found. As long as we were moving, things were less likely to go wrong. With young dogs most problems occur when you stop, their lines get tangled, or they get into a hassle with the dogs around them. The chances of losing the sled are also highest when you are dealing with such problems, so I was afraid to stop.

But it seemed like everyone else in the race was resting in the woods. I started growing disgusted with my fear of stopping, but just could not do it. On and on I went, arguing with myself each time I passed up a good spot to park. I knew I must have gone past Jeff by now and his warning rang in my ears.

"Do not pass me!"

He had said it in a joking manner, but I knew what he had meant. He had lectured me repeatedly that it was impossible to go too slow during the first few days, especially if you were a rookie. He wanted me to take lots of rests and slow the team down as much as possible. The race could not be won in the first few days, but it could be lost. It was a common mistake, in all the excitement, to run the dogs too far and too fast.

And I did not want to race; I had no dreams of grandeur. I simply wanted to succeed. I was afraid to stop moving, afraid to step off the runners. Afraid, afraid, afraid.

By the time I finally stopped, the dogs were moving really slowly because of the afternoon heat. My best parking choice was, by then, behind a couple thin, nearly branchless black spruce trees. I was filled with self-loathing thinking about the coolness of the woods I had traveled through earlier. My first big lesson had been learned: if nearly every other musher in the race was doing something, it was probably a good idea.

Just after I had finished handing out snacks, Palmer Sagoonik pulled up. He was from Shaktoolik and was a relative of Chief, a close friend of mine whose dad had come from Siberia. Adopted at the turn of the century by a Native woman, Chief's dad, like most of the next three generations, had lived off the reindeer herds they carefully shepherded around the tundra.

As an Iditarod volunteer one year, we had waited for mushers to arrive in Shaktoolik, and Palmer had explained how he had lost most of his reindeer the previous fall. A large migrating herd of caribou had moved through the area, and once mixed together with his herd, they were impossible to separate again. As he spoke I had marveled at his tone of voice. There was no anger, just simple regret. It was just an act of nature, an act of God.

When I first met him, Palmer had a very small team of sled dogs. As he spoke of them, he moved to the edge of his chair and the timbre of his voice changed. He seemed anxious to talk to anyone interested in huskies, and I imagined his opportunities were limited in the tiny local population. During one of the previous races he had hung up a small, hand-lettered sign in the checkpoint.

"Wanted: old or retired Iditarod sled dogs."

Several mushers had sent dogs back to Shaktoolik after finishing their race to help Palmer start breeding a competitive team. I had felt sorry for him when he shyly admitted he dreamed of running the Iditarod someday. I knew how expensive it was, how the cost kept many people living in remote villages from competing, but somehow he had done it. I had proudly been with his family in Nome when he had completed his rookie year at fifty-four years old.

Palmer had spoken to me several times in the last few days—gentle words of encouragement, always in the careful measured cadence of village English I so loved. Unlike my crazy puppies, his team now stood still when he told them to stop. Briefly, he leaned on his handle bow and nodded over at my team with subtle advice.

"Pretty nice group you have. Too hot, though. Take it nice and slow."

I pulled into Yenta Station at 6:30 in the evening and decided to rest the team five hours. I had spent the night here on a training run in February and knew the warm hospitality of the lodge owners. Jeff and Donna's oldest daughter, Cali, had wanted to practice on the trail that she would be running in the Junior Iditarod, and had invited Tyrell Seavey, the current champion, along for the adventure. Of course, parents being parents, no one was going to let two teenagers go on an overnight trip alone, so Tyrell had brought along his little brother, and I had been invited for good measure. Taking four large dog teams on a date made it pretty different from your typical dinner and a movie!

As soon as I parked my team, I realized the handle to my cooker was already broken. Only 115 miles into the race and one of my main pieces of equipment was broken, and I hadn't even entered the Alaska Range!

The cooker was a two-piece unit, one of the most important things I was carrying in my sled. A five-gallon metal bucket had been modified with holes and wire to hold another smaller pot above a four-inch air space at the bottom. A small amount of Heet poured into the bottom burned and produced enough heat to boil water in the nested pot. Every single meal the dogs consumed over the next two weeks, and most of mine as well, depended on this contraption working correctly.

I carried it up to the log cabin and, embarrassed, showed it to the family. The kids all looked seriously concerned, and when the father swooped it from my arms, they solemnly followed him out to the shop. Kids growing up in the Bush, like kids on farms, often have a wealth of knowledge, but more importantly confidence in tackling whatever life presents them. Their daily lives are filled with little challenges, and though it is sometimes hard to pinpoint their skills, on a sinking ship I would choose them to be in my lifeboat.

I sat down to a steaming plate of spaghetti the mother offered me and nodded to Hans Gatt, who was just finishing his. He was on a winning streak, having just won both the Copper Basin 300 and the Yukon Quest, a remarkable feat, but suddenly as a rookie, I couldn't think of a single intelligent thing to say to him. I was grateful when the patriarch of the house returned, and his son was proudly carrying the mended cooker. I tried to thank him, but he quickly shrugged me off. Extreme shyness was also a common trait of people who lived in the Bush for a long time.

I pulled the hook around noon, and we followed the Yentna River for nearly the entire thirty-five miles to the next checkpoint in the village of Skwentna. It was an easy run, but the excitement of the last days had tuckered out my puppies. They slept sprawled on their mounds of straw. I crawled into a corner of Joe Delia's house, but couldn't really sleep. I had studied pictures of this house and our host for years in Iditarod publications. I wanted to talk to Joe about being a postmaster in this community of twenty-five. I wanted to tell him about my neighbor Linda and how the mail plane is supposed to come once a week, but rarely makes it more than once every couple weeks. I knew he would relate, but it was also close to 4:00 A.M. when I finished doing my chores.

I immediately realized the next morning when the first rays of sun began to threaten a warm day that I should have planned on leaving sooner. Finger Lake was forty-five miles away, and we quickly ate up the first miles, following the river and then a series of swamps. When we started to climb the Shell Hills, I really began to feel the heat. The team was moving fine, but I was concerned about Coco, my big coastal dog. His thick coat was much better suited for the stormy country around Nome than a warm spring day in the foothills of the Alaska Range.

Coco had only been added to my team the night before we left Anchorage. Reno had been bitten in the parking lot. It wasn't serious, but it had made him lame, and regrettably I decided to replace him with Coco. Reno and I had spent nearly every night together during the past two winters; I had been the first ever to put a harness on him. When I had woken in terror during the months leading up to the race, it had been his furry neck I had used to muffle my sobs. Leaving him behind in Anchorage had been really hard, but luckily there had been no time to dwell on it.

I didn't know Coco as well, and consequently by the time I got to Finger Lake, I had decided to drop him. Maybe it was just the heat making him lethargic, but at any rate he just didn't seem enthusiastic enough to stay with the team. During the race, mushers will drop dogs for a variety of reasons. Because an unhappy dog cannot be forced to contribute, leaving Coco was an easy decision. I had fifteen others who were thrilled to be running this trail.

Another kerfuffle changed my schedule, though, and I ended up staying overnight at the Finger Lake checkpoint. Shuman, my muscled wheel dog, had picked another fight that had left him with a puncture in his front leg. The vet who examined my team said if I was leaving immediately it was best to drop him, but with a little extra time and effort, he might be able to stay with the team.

I liked Shuman, though his fires often kept me hopping. He pulled so damn hard I certainly didn't want to lose him this early in the race. Besides, he was one of the best singers in the team; all season I had been able to get him to howl by merely hinting tunes from the soundtrack from *Call of the Wild*. I settled into a long night of massaging his sore wrist, then alternating between ice and heat packs, chiding him like a naughty kid brother, cooing tough love. I didn't mind staying extra-long at the checkpoint, I told him, but it'd better be worth it.

CHAPTER 17

An Iditarod Twist

*I*t was worth it.

Between massages, I climbed the hill to the lodge. Everyone else was sleeping except for Doug Swingley, who sat alone at the long dining-room table. I had seen him earlier, and sensed there was oddness to the reigning champion being at the same checkpoint as a rookie like me, but really hadn't thought more about it.

Mr. Swingley had been enjoying a winning streak that was baffling and infuriating many Alaskans. For the past three years, he had won the race with such ease that it had made the race almost . . . boring. His leads were so huge, and attitude so casual, that there was almost a fury about wanting to beat him. As a checker, I had spoken to him several times, but had silently agreed. His confidence was disturbing and I, too, had avoided dealing with him whenever possible.

Now, though, in the middle of the night, armored in the bliss of being on the trail as a musher, I eased into a chair across from him. I pulled off my beaver hat and scratched my bangs into order, then nodded a greeting. The lights were so low I could barely make out his profile. He was just a skinny guy in long underwear who happened to be famous.

"I have a question for you, Doug," I said, removing my boots and easing my feet up on the chair beside me. "Rather, I'd like you to confirm a story I have heard."

He raised an eyebrow and casually straightened the sleeve of his sweater. He had sewn pockets across the chest for keeping spare headlamp batteries warm during the long runs.

"But you must promise not to tell me if it is wrong."

His expression, so trained to deal with strangers and the media, went from confident to controlled puzzlement. I smiled. "I don't want you blowing my fantasies." He leaned back, tilting his head to look down on me.

"I have a crush on your brother."

For years, the Swingley brothers had been partners in a very successful dog-breeding program. Greg's skills had initially been better known than his older brother's, though winning the Iditarod, not once, but four times, had put Doug alone in the spotlight. I had never met the sibling and really had no desire to, but had once heard a good story that I really wanted to believe.

In 1998, Greg had won the Kuskokwim 300, one of the toughest dog races in the world. Not particularly a surprise considering the talents of the young Swingley, it was nevertheless an exciting accomplishment. Mushers are required to attend a banquet in Bethel where the awards are given, and each racer has the opportunity to speak to an audience. When it was his time, Greg Swingley stepped up to the microphone, beaming. With a roguish grin, he called all the other mushers forward to the stage. Carefully looking over his fellow competitors lined up in front of the room, he said, "I'm not very often in this position, and I have a request." The little room was crowded, but quickly fell silent at the champion's words.

"I would like everyone to raise their arms over their heads and do a plié."

Bethel sits on the Kuskokwim River downriver from the village of Kwethluk, upriver from Napakiak and basically north of Eek. Most of the locals are Yup'ik Eskimo. In this tough little village four hundred miles from the closest performing arts center, ballet must have seemed as foreign as scuba diving. I imagined the shock wave that likely passed through the collection of modern-day ruffians gathered in the room and had to smile.

Greg Swingley bred good sled dogs, but also happened to teach ballet in Montana. I never wanted to meet him—there was no way he could live up to my expectations.

Doug now chuckled. I could tell, as soon as he began, that he was a good storyteller, and together we laughed as he recounted the tale. Not surprisingly, there had been resistance from some of the dog drivers and, following the tradition of the Masters, Greg had been tough on them. He had rapped knees that weren't positioned wide enough. He had demanded that arms be raised with the correct amount of curve. Fingertips had to touch, toes—though housed in giant snow boots—had to point. Chins had to be held at just the right angle. This was the second time I had been told he was actually mean to the ones who did not comply fully or quickly enough.

John Baker, Rick Swenson, Jeff King, Charlie Boulding; these were not only some of the top mushers in the world, but they were some of the toughest individuals as well. Looking at any of them would have naturally brought images of the rugged pioneers who had come to this land in search of gold—beards, wrinkles, dirty clothes—and yet under Greg's strict instructions, they had become meek children, obediently bending to his will. Nureyev would have been proud. Personally I considered it a great moment in Alaskan history.

At the end of his story, I stood up, shaking my head. It was even better than I had imagined. I had worried for years that it was somehow not true. Doug now looked around the dark room. Everyone else was either sleeping or tending to their dogs.

"Are you curious why I am here?"

I shrugged. "I figured everyone else had already asked," I said. Actually, I had thought very little about it. I had been concentrating on Shuman's injury and dropping Coco. Interestingly enough, after carefully following the race for years, I now had very little concern for the front-runners.

"I'm in forty-second place," he said and when I didn't react he leaned forward across the table with an impish grin on his face.

"I've retired."

I sat back down.

"I am not competing this year."

For a moment, I stared. How could this be? This was the man everyone had spent years trying to beat. He had worn and flaunted the Iditarod crown like nothing else mattered in the world. I carefully studied his expression, then slowly shook my head.

"Really?" I sucked in my breath to divert a grin. *Unbelievable.* But still on my guard, I squinted at him in the dark, "That's pretty funny."

Doug had been winning the Iditarod with such apparent ease; it really had taken some of the fun out of the race. There had been talk and strategy all winter—all over the state—about how to defeat this unbeatable Montanan. The newspapers were full of interviews, and the consensus was that it would be nearly impossible to beat his present team. The typical interviews with Doug had taken place right up to the start of the race. Cocky, self-assured, he was returning with his sixteen champions and nothing could stop him.

"I think everybody knows it's going to take somebody doing something special to beat me," he had bragged at a prerace interview.

"I'm retiring from competitive mushing," he now said mischievously. All winter it had been a well-guarded secret, but it would be in the press by morning.

I silently slapped my hand on the table, and threw my head back grinning at the ceiling. Outside the window, ten feet of snow covered the ground and a dozen dog teams slept. This was so typical Iditarod, this bizarre and delightful twist. The whole field had decided Doug had some innovative new scheme for winning the race—that he had stayed behind the leaders with a devious plan in mind. No one yet knew that the main competitor had his boots off and was preparing for another long nap.

"Your boss," he said, "will have no idea until some time tomorrow morning, when he reaches Nikolai."

I quickly realized Jeff was doing the run out of Rohn on his way to Nikolai. He was probably somewhere in the Farewell Burn right now. Nearly a hundred-mile stretch. It was true, being out of communication for close to fourteen hours, he would be one of the last to know. I looked at Doug and we both laughed. Jeff had probably seen Doug's location on the time sheet before leaving Rohn. He would likely have spent the run second-guessing the reigning champion's game plan.

It would have been fun to be the one to tell him, but I knew Jeff. There would be no satisfaction in his response. While in race mode, Jeff showed very few emotions. He sorted incoming information, dropping superfluous details. His total focus was on his dog team and the closest competitors. Though he may have spent the long run attempting to decipher the Montanan's plan, there would be no lingering over the new facts. Doug would simply no longer be his main rival. Someone else would take his place. The story would only matter or be of interest after the card game was completely over.

Doug wanted to take his time doing the Iditarod Trail this year, something he had never been able to do. He was traveling with friends from Montana: the kid training his puppy team and a couple who also had teams of young dogs. He wanted to meet the people in the villages along the way, to thank the volunteers. He wanted to see the countryside he had missed always traveling so quickly. He wanted to enjoy the trail. This was the most incredible dog team of his career, and he wanted to enjoy feeling them sprint from checkpoint to checkpoint.

"This is my victory lap," he beamed.

My own adventure awaited me, though, and finally I searched out a secluded corner to lie down among the other sleeping mushers. I felt giddy, and though I needed to rest, felt no desire. I had never once thought that any part of the Iditarod was going to be fun—this had never been even a remote consideration—and yet here I was on the eve of doing the Dalzell Gorge, happier than I could imagine. Death or serious injury may await me in the next twenty-four hours, but so be it. As Doug passed me on the way to his own corner of the room, I whispered, as much to myself as to him.

"Brilliant, absolutely brilliant."

CHAPTER 18

Chilling Advice

I lay down at Finger Lake for only a couple of hours. I was up again by 3:30 in the morning. After having a vet agree that Shuman was in fine shape to travel, I pulled out of Finger Lake before the first hints of morning had grazed the sky. After fourteen hours of rest, my team was once again the crazy puppies I loved to fear. The trail was wild for the first several miles, twisting through the woods that surrounded us so tightly that I was constantly ducking under branches as I hopped back and forth on the sled's runners. I knew the Happy River Steps were coming, but no one had warned me about this snaky part of the ride. It was exciting as hell, and since I did not hit anything, I had to admit the adrenalin rush was actually fun.

I didn't see the Steps coming, so didn't have time to work myself up into a frenzy. I began plunging down a series of switchbacks, diving down grades I would never, ever voluntarily take my team in training. I had small LED lights on the collars of the leaders, so at least I had some forewarning each time they fell away from the beam of my headlamp—either down the trail or around a sharp turn. It took only several minutes, and we skidded to the bottom of the two-hundred-foot drop without a single mishap. I knew the heavy snowfall had padded this notoriously difficult part of the trail, but was it really possible *that* was the Happy River Steps?

A short while later, as the dusk of morning was just beginning to turn into true light, I came sliding down onto Puntilla Lake and into the Rainy

Pass checkpoint thirty miles farther down the Iditarod Trail. Teams were parked neatly in rows along the lake, and someone led me to the far end of the pack. I would have a clear shot back out onto the trail. After setting my hook, I was surprised at the sudden tranquillity. Though there were probably close to a hundred dogs nearby, most were sleeping or watching the setting from their beds of straw. The mushers were quietly working on their gear or napping on their sleds. It was so peaceful.

I quickly snacked the dogs, and then hiked to the stacks of straw and drop bags. It was a long way down the lake and I was relieved to see there was a plastic sled to use for hauling the gear. I hadn't bothered to take off my heavy insulated suit and was still shaking with the excitement from the run. I passed Doug on the way back to my team and he smiled.

"A little hairy leaving Finger, huh? Guess we could have left a little later when there was more daylight to see the trail."

I hesitated. My run had been like a dream and I resisted waking up. Finally I shook my head, a little embarrassed. I shyly confessed. "It was perfect—absolutely perfect."

By the time I got back to my sled, I was sweating. The dogs were already curled up in the warm sunshine, looking very much like youngsters. I set about unpacking my drop bag and arranging everything into piles around my sled. I could only find two of the three bags I had sent out to the checkpoint, which meant I was missing some important ingredients for the dogs' diet. From my years of volunteering, I knew this was just a reality on such a complicated long race, and had already talked to Kelly Williams about borrowing some meat. I had proposed a trade of chocolate for tripe, and she seemed interested.

"I love Alaska, and I love the Iditarod!" I exclaimed to a tourist who had remained at my side through my early chores. He was sweet and I wanted to return the kindness by giving him "inside" tidbits about being in the race.

"My headlamp hit a branch," I said. "It twisted my hat so I couldn't see and I hit a tree." I set out bowls in the snow for the dogs' meal and began ladling the chunky stew. "It was wild but I didn't let go."

He laughed gently and shook his head. He was afraid to bother me with too many questions, but delighted with every word. He was following the race with his wife. They were camped in a tent at the edge of the makeshift runway. They weren't young, and the image impressed me. It was at least −10°F.

"Where are you going next?" I asked.

"Takotna."

"Oh, you'll love Takotna."

I set a bowl of food in front of Bismarck, who delicately pulled out a single chunk of meat. Portland sunk his nose into his dish, instantly inhaling everything. "It's famous for its pies," I said. "All the mushers want to go there for the pies." For a moment I hesitated, looking down at the bowl of dog food before me in the snow, and then quietly added, "I hope I make it that far."

Looking worried, the man studied my face, and then smiled kindly. I thought of Virgil and all the encouraging words he had given me over the past few months. I could almost feel him cheering me on from back at the kennel.

"Takotna sure can't be prettier than this," the man said softly.

We looked up around us. This checkpoint, a cluster of log cabins, was nestled in a valley surrounded by sharp-peaked mountains that gleamed in the bright sunshine. Dogs were sleeping in neat little rows, and mushers casually went about their chores. I had to agree. To a rookie in the Iditarod, nothing in the world could be prettier than Rainy Pass.

After doing everything I could think of for my team, I walked down the length of the lake to the official manned checkpoint. Rather than continuing to fuss over them, I knew I needed to leave the dogs to their rest. Though not the least bit hungry myself, I also knew I needed calories.

The checker was Jim Johnson, a volunteer I had worked with several times. Nearly fifteen hundred volunteers were needed to make this race across the wilderness possible; many saved their precious vacation time for the first two weeks in March. They gave up trips to Europe or Hawaii, or visits with the in-laws, to answer phones, haul supplies, and escort dog teams down Fourth Avenue in Anchorage. Many had been volunteering for more than a decade—people who would never be interested in stepping onto the runners of a dogsled themselves, but were passionate about any aspect of the event. From working with Jim, I knew he was one of the most dedicated volunteers on the trail.

It was fun to get a hug, and I gratefully took the Styrofoam cup of coffee he offered. I sat down with a sandwich and a stack of granola bars, joining the mushers from Montana. I was not tired, but it felt good to sink into the couch.

Harmony and Jason sat next to each other. I gathered they were a couple from the way they shared tidbits of food. Daniel, who was training a team of puppies for Doug Swingley, looked more like a choirboy than a dog musher. Blushed from the early morning run, everyone had shy grins of delight and crazy hairdos from the hats that lay at their feet. The woodstove scented the cabin like Christmas morning, and Harmony's laughter followed every comment, encouraging the group into a playful banter.

"Normally when I sit here, everyone is glaring at each other," said Doug, "sizing each other up."

He stretched luxuriously, balancing his socked feet on the edge of the closest chair. He smiled smugly and I had to turn away to hide my own grin. I had seen that haughty smile at checkpoints, and in race publications, for years. Now it seemed completely different.

"But we don't care!" said Harmony gaily.

Playfully I cut her off. "Of course we care—we're sizing each other up!" I let my voice whine a little. "I know we're all trying to figure out who is going to be first to leave!"

"Oh yeah—I want someone else to go first. I just don't want anyone to see me get dragged down the hills!" Her laughter was contagious and she did not seem frightened at all, just delighted. "I am carrying my toothbrush so I can have nice-smelling breath for the autopsy."

Doug began describing the trail that lay ahead of us all. Jason had done the Iditarod before, but Harmony, Karen, and I were rookies, and we listened with occasional gasps.

"I don't think I have ever dragged between here and Rohn," he said. I was surprised; was he hinting that he too sometimes flipped his sled? I had never imagined him out of control—ever. "It's back there at the Happy River, the snow is deep and the sleds tip over because of the deep ruts," he said, lacing his fingers around a cup of coffee. "The Dalzell Gorge is not quite so whoop-de-do."

"What about . . . you said that right turn, past that tree?" Harmony pursed her lips. I realized she knew more about the trail than I did.

"What tree?" I asked. Doug looked past me at Harmony.

"Well that thing could be dug out some, but there really isn't that much snow. Here, there is ten feet of snow and it can make those two-foot-deep crevasses. The Dalzell Gorge is just really steep, with lots of tight turning across boulders and snow bridges."

"What tree?" I insisted, and Harmony turned toward me.

"Oh, he says there's a big spruce tree with notches about eight feet off the ground." Her statement hung in the air for a moment.

Though I knew what was coming, I couldn't resist asking Doug, "Why do people stop and notch the tree?" Suddenly, I was having flashbacks and remembered hearing part of this scenario from Jeff.

In mid-February, we had loaded our food drop bags onto Jeff's flatbed trailer and hauled them to Anchorage. I had decided this would be a great time for Jeff to describe the Iditarod Trail in detail. He was a great storyteller. I had often wondered if this had been developed through years of remote living, having a house with no television reception, standing around campfires with friends. Fishers are often good storytellers as well, and I knew it came from the close companionship of living in tight quarters for long periods. I loved the ritual and was a good listener.

Jeff had traveled the Iditarod Trail every March for the last fourteen years, and his calculating mind did not miss a detail. He had once told me that a rookie could never really be competitive in the race. The advantage of knowing exactly where you were in the overall scheme of things was substantial. Distance to checkpoints, rivers, difficult parts of the trail, places where you could relax—all of these added up to be decisive factors on how you managed the dog team. Experienced Iditarod veterans often rested their dogs in the same spot, tying to the same tree year after year. They knew the landmarks so well they could gauge their speed and make minor adjustments to arrive right on the schedule they wanted.

As soon as Jeff began talking, I realized it would be information overload. In the fading light, I took as many notes as possible. At first it was easy, both his descriptions and the trail I followed through his words. I was able to ask questions and make lighthearted comments. I could see the sloughs, the flat, open swamps, and the holes in the Skwentna River. As we gradually climbed, though, deeper into the Alaska Range, I began to feel physically ill.

Very steep corners, skirting a canyon, difficult trail—he started talking about losing sight of the team because some of the turns were so tight, and I became first hot, then cold, and then dizzy.

"Get off the brake, have faith there is a trail," he said evenly, and I was grateful the truck had grown dark. Tears started creeping down my face and I tried to rattle papers to cover the sound of me trying to hold back my running nose.

"Don't stop . . . look for signs . . . the scariest part is the side-hilling—don't tip over . . . narrow canyon—you may get wet—you may have to lay the sled on its side to slow it down . . . glare ice . . . snaking through the woods . . . the markers here are always gone." I knew he was not trying to scare me, though I suspected he could read my silences. Somewhere near Ophir, I threw down my pen and blurted out, "Enough!"

I had meant it to sound gay and perhaps confident, but the tone was off. Suddenly the sound of the windshield wipers filled the cab of the truck. I knew by his not making a joke about it that he understood perfectly well. We traveled the rest of the hours into the city in silence. At one point Jeff patted my shoulder.

"If you want to talk about anything, I'm here," he said. But even seeing a moose on the shoulder of the highway could not entice my lips to move.

Doug now smiled almost sadly. "They don't stop and notch the trees—at least not on purpose. The tree is at Moose Creek, right at the very top of the gorge. Sleds have been slamming into that same tree for thirty years."

Harmony patted me on the knee and let loose with one of her nervous laughs. "When you see that tree you're getting ready to have some fun."

"I'm just trying to prepare you for how you're going to feel!" Doug said.

"Oh, I know how I'm going to feel," she laughed.

"You're going to go over Rainy Pass and down through this windy brush into creek drainage, and it's going to feel like the Happy River Steps. Two, three miles of that and then you come out onto this pristine river bottom, and you're going to think, 'Oh, yeah, I made it through the Dalzell.' Then a mile or so further, the trail takes a hard left and goes up this little hill. You will think it is the steepest hill you have ever seen; it feels like going up a hill on a roller coaster: *ka-chink, ka-chink, ka-chink.*" He narrowed his eyes, showing laugh lines, and his cheeks were rosy as he grinned at us. He was having fun.

"I feel sick," I said.

"And you'll go around this spruce tree and straight, and I mean straight, down this hill." He cleared his throat. "You have just entered the Dalzell Gorge."

The little group was silent, and I could hear a dog barking down on the lake. Finally, Harmony's musical voice cut the tension. "How far from the ka-chink ka-chink to the whoop-de—whoop-de-whew?"

Doug lowered his voice and for the first time I sensed compassion in his tone. "About four miles." he said.

I caught Karen's eye as I turned to hide my expression. Four miles. We could put on a brave front, but we were all scared to death. One wrong move here could finish your Iditarod.

A small group of children came in at that moment and Doug congenially posed and signed autographs. I bit resolutely into another granola bar and smiled over at Harmony. "I sent out e-mails looking for people to pull the plug if I get hurt beyond repair in the Gorge," I said. "My Blue Cross is paid, and the plug-pullers are lined up." She giggled, but nervously turned away.

Doug started talking about staying at the Bear Creek shelter cabin halfway between Rohn and Nikolai. The run needed a break halfway, so why not find the cabin and do it in style? I remembered hearing about it from the volunteer Trailbreakers; it was off the Iditarod Trail by about a mile.

"I've been by there, but there weren't any tracks going in," said Doug, and Harmony loudly scoffed.

"Of course not—you're usually in front of everyone else!"

"What are you going to do about straw?" asked Jason. I could tell he was into logistics. He looked to be in his early thirties, wiry and compact, though his voice was surprisingly deep.

"Oh, we're the tail-enders—I bet they have extra straw," Doug said.

I turned in mock horror to Karen. "We're tail-enders?" Though as a volunteer I had always enjoyed and respected the mushers in the back of the pack, even more so than the front-runners, there was a stigma to being behind so many other racers.

"I just found out I was in forty-ninth place!" Doug said proudly. "So at least we're not last."

The talk then turned to the unfortunates who had scratched in the race and, for a moment, the room grew somber. For those of us who did not really understand or couldn't even really imagine all that lay ahead of us, "scratch" was a depressingly sickening term. I was sorry to hear Burt Bomhoff had scratched. He had seemed like a sweet man when I met him on the runway in Rohn my first year. Now I was doing the Iditarod myself, while he, the one with thirty years of experience, had already scratched. G. B. Jones, who had parked behind me on the lake, had hit a tree. His face was a bloody mess. Anything could go wrong. Any one of us might not make it.

Doug seemed to want to break the dark spell and, counting on his fingers, he announced. "Aren't we going to be a pretty sight charging into Nome? By tonight we may be approaching a fourth of the way there."

"A journey of a thousand miles begins with one step," said Jason.

Surprisingly I found myself almost gushing. "Who cares how long it takes, if it continues like this? Who would ever possibly want it to end?" All of them were shaking their heads in agreement. We all had had perfect runs so far and were obviously feeling the same way. The mother with the children came back in, leading a shy child by the hand. She apologized to Doug, asking for just one more picture, but he took her hand and put his arm over the boy's shoulder.

"Don't worry; this is what it's all about. That's why I'm back here."

CHAPTER 19

Alone and Yet Not

I pulled out of Rainy Pass at midafternoon. I wanted to leave early enough to run the Gorge in some kind of daylight. I was as frightened as I could possibly be and still be able to stand upright. The moment I had stepped back outside the shelter and the company at the checkpoint, I had felt dizzy with fear and a profound loneliness. I had sat in the straw with Lassen, stroking her head and letting the hot flashes of panic cool beneath my snowsuit. I nuzzled the velvet insides of her ears and she stretched lazily in her straw bed. I watched with wonder as she slowly nodded off with a single paw resting on my thigh. When I stood and began the final chores before pulling the hook, I was absolutely calm and methodical—and totally numb.

As I began the climb up the pass, the beauty and realization of what I was doing lulled me into a stupor. I had dreaded and dreamed of this moment so many times, it felt more like a rerun than reality.

We climbed, ever higher and higher. The crisp sharpness of the air scrubbed away any smells. We were above most vegetation, and higher than where animals willingly went. It seemed as if we were in a wide valley, but what showed of the mountains surrounding us were the windblown peaks—the raw summits of the Alaska Range. We weren't looking up at these fabulous crowns from afar—we were on them. I tried to imagine how anyone had first found this trail through the top of the world.

The dogs were so serious pulling. Salem never looked back as he led us, and Lassen stared at the ground concentrating, the muscles of her backsides working hard under her honey-colored coat. Shuman and Latte were straining so hard in wheel position that the sled felt almost empty. Bismarck was all eyes, looking at the crests of the mountains, the odd boulders, the feathery brush; he was the first to alert me someone was behind us.

The Montanans had pulled out of the checkpoint just after me—Doug leading the pack—and now he was fast approaching me on the trail. I would have been bummed about a team catching me with such a steady gain, but it was Doug Swingley, after all. This was the team that had won the last year's Iditarod with Doug, and likely the year before and the one before that. These were some of the finest canine athletes in the world. His famous dog Peppy was undoubtedly in that team somewhere; my guys weren't even two years old yet.

"Do you want the trail?" I called back to him. His parka seemed almost familiar by now, but he nodded all businesslike. There was no trace of the camaraderie shown during the last few hours at the checkpoint. Doug was on the trail. His team powered past my puppies with so much force I could tell they were swayed. We all stared as the team disappeared over the ridge. Bless their hearts; they were already working so hard.

Actually once he was out of sight, I was not interested in going fast any more. The Gorge would be upon us all too soon. If life as I knew it was going to change, I wanted to delay it as long as possible.

We climbed higher and dropped down some steep plunges. I tried not to get my hopes up that I was beyond somewhere I was not, and my hands began to cramp from holding the handle bow so tight. The little challenges came as almost a relief, breaking the tension, covering the silence of the gloomy passage. The wide pass narrowed to a final narrow slit that allowed passage through these formidable mountains. The sun did not reach into these icy depths; the rocks and snow were a single frozen substance in their earthly armor. I felt very alone and suddenly afraid for my naïve youngsters working so hard just ahead of me. Spared the stories, they knew not what they were getting into.

Ka-chink, ka-chink, ka-chink—I heard it as we slowly climbed, indeed, the steepest hill I could imagine going up. Doug had described it well. However, it was over before the suffering went on too long. The bow of my sled just barely missed the famed spruce tree as we dove over the edge and down into the Gorge. For a fleeting moment I had the satisfaction I hadn't added to the depth of the notch. In the next instant, I was plunged into the rocky evils of a narrow canyon with little hope of staying with my team.

Here the trail winds back and forth across Dalzell Creek, traversing a series of ice bridges that the Iditarod Trailbreakers carefully construct just for the race. With nearly a thousand miles of trail, each one is a small miracle of salvation—how could strangers be so caring? This harrowing passageway would be impossible without the dedication of these unrecognized volunteers.

The Gorge opened briefly into a fantasy field of large trees. Though I had been warned, I couldn't help but wish—again—that I were already past what I knew lay ahead. For a brief moment, I unclamped my grip on the sled, and pushed my hat down further on my head. Then, around a placid corner and like a cruel joke, I immediately shot back into a rocky hall, twisting across ninety-degree turns back and forth across the creek. The creek itself devilishly snaked its way down the canyon, frozen sharp with razor-edged caverns. These ugly, dark holes loomed first on our left, and then on our right as we crisscrossed our way down, threatening to suck the team in on every curve.

I smacked some trees hard, slammed into boulders, and once lost my grip on the handle bow. Both the sled and I went up, forward, and down, at the same speed—though we were totally separated in mid-flight. Luckily, the trail at this moment was as steep as it was appalling. I was shocked to find the handle bow shoved back into my hands and, with some measure of gratitude, held on for dear life.

Dear life. How many times did I nearly lose my dear life in those long miles? Countless. I could have been crippled a hundred times. My head could have been smashed a dozen more. I survived only through some kind of miracle. When I again lost my grip—and for an eternity was separated from my sled and team—it was an act of providence that put that root, or rock, or tussock, or whatever it was that pinned one of the sled runners. Some guardian held it for those few precious seconds it took for me to sprint forward and jump back on the suicide train.

I did not know it, but when Salem finally missed a turn, and led the team off the trail—into the creek itself—I was just minutes from completing the slalom course. However, what I did know was that things had gone from bad to seriously worse.

Dalzell Créek itself is not terribly deep, but neither is it totally frozen over. The water continues to slice into the rock well after winter has set in; sheer velocity keeps much of it from ever freezing, and the frozen edges cave in like a serrated knife zigzagging down the canyon. Parts of it look like the trail itself, so it was understandable when the leaders missed seeing the ice bridge and turned down into what looked like a trail.

There was not a doubt in my mind that if we continued, someone would get hurt badly, and instinctively I flipped the sled onto its side. I threw all my weight into making it stop. There were several sickening cracks as we smacked hard into boulders but finally we jerked to a halt.

Ahead of me, the creek sharply dropped, and I could see holes where the dogs could have easily broken a leg, jagged holes where I could have snapped a bone or cracked my skull. I stomped my snow hook into some ice and, shaking badly, crept forward to the front of the team. I knew I needed to get them back on the trail while they were still all a little shocked from the last several miles. Keeping my voice calm, I dragged them toward the missed ice bridge.

Generally, ice bridges are made by cutting lengths of tree branches and stacking them the width of the creek. After building a sturdy base, snow is then shoveled on top and jammed into the cracks, creating a smooth, safe surface. The Gorge is famous for needing so many of these bridges that often the Trailbreakers spend several days in the area working on just this four-mile section of trail. Every year, though, the spring floods sweep away all their handiwork and the trail disappears once again back into the wilds.

Just as I got the team lined back out onto the trail, I heard an odd yelp and turned with horror to see that Alto had jumped Shasta. She was in full heat—and thrilled to have him. In one split instant, my chances of getting through this nightmare in daylight were gone. Once the mating process has begun, it is nearly impossible to separate dogs for at least half an hour, and I knew I could not move the team. This was such an absolute certainty that I felt no panic, just total acceptance.

I pulled the sled as far off the trail as I could to wait out the love encounter. As the woods darkened around me, I tried to keep my voice normal as I spoke to the dogs. Jason and Harmony flew by on their teams, obviously still intact, though both grunted opinions about the trail. Karen showed up and I was delighted when she decided to wait for me. The bit of sky I could see through the canyon had turned from a soft rose to pitch black and I nervously tightened the strap of my headlamp. What if I lost the team in the dark?

The moment the lovers separated, I called back to Karen. I rechecked my headlamp and pulled the hook. In some ways, the darkness was good because I couldn't see what lay on either side of the trail. I took several hard hits without knowing what waited just outside my beam of light. It was a surprise, several minutes later, when I found myself sliding down a chute and onto the glare ice of the Tatina River. *It was over? Had we done it? We made it through the Dalzell Gorge!?*

I heard Karen's laugh as she, too, skidded onto the ice in the darkness. We skated the last miles along the river under the earliest stars of the evening. It was too fast and nerve-wracking, but I howled into the night air when the trail paralleled the Rohn airstrip. I knew exactly where I was; I had really made it through the Alaska Range. I was alive! I could still walk! I still had my team! No one was hurt!

I flashed on the first time I had landed at the airstrip as a volunteer and shook my head at the wonder of it. Only four years had passed, and yet here I was driving my own dog team. Jasper would soon officially check me into Rohn, with Terry parking me in the woods I knew so well. I had to take some deep breaths to prepare myself; I did not want to start blubbering in front of everyone.

The dogs smelled the wood smoke, so they were virtually charging when I stepped on the brake in front of the Rohn cabin. I had to hug my friends before signing the paperwork, but there was no time for small talk. My team was hungry, and I knew the walk to the river for water would take more time than I wanted. However, there was a comfort in knowing all of this. With the excitement of the last couple days, it was a relief to spend the night in a familiar place.

I found two buckets and, putting them on a plastic sled, quickly started the long walk back down the trail to get water. Some people melted snow, while others even attempted sending ice out to Rohn in their drop bags, but most people did the lonely trudge back to the airstrip and then down a narrow path to the river.

One year, Harry Caldwell, a musher from Wasilla, had just returned from the river with two buckets of hard-earned water. Right in front of the cabin a snag in the trail tipped the plastic sled, spilling the precious liquid. He was tired and he must have been hungry as well, and wanting to finish his chores—yet his response was classic Harry.

"Guess I'll go get some more!" he said cheerfully and turned right back around. For many it was these little challenges that exposed the depth of their character. I had never looked at Harry again without smiling.

The steps leading down to the river were just as I remembered— carefully carved into the snowbank. I had helped make similar ones with Terry, digging for hours and then pouring water over them to freeze into a solid staircase. As I shifted my bucket, water splashed onto my pant leg, instantly encasing my leg in an armor of ice, but I didn't worry. I knew the fire in the cabin would be hot.

When I returned to my team, I gratefully shared my water with Karen, who had just pulled into the checkpoint. My walk had refreshed me, erasing the post-Gorge daze that I could still see in her eyes. "We did it, Karen! We survived the Dalzell! We are alive and we are in Rohn."

She looked down at her dogs and then up at the trees that surrounded us. She mumbled something and exhaled a sigh. I wondered if I had been in her position if I would have had the class, the courage, to risk doing what she had done for me in the Gorge, but shamefully didn't voice my doubts. Impulsively I threw my arms around her shoulders.

"Thank you so much for waiting for me."

CHAPTER 20

No, the Insane Part Isn't Over Yet

*K*aren and I were moving slowly and stiffly by the time our chores were done and we entered the Rohn cabin. It was –20°F outside, and the steamy heat that enveloped me inside the cabin had me feeling deliciously thickheaded and off balance. I caught the barest hint of perfume—perhaps it was even someone's deodorant—and flashed on how a fresh pillowcase would smell and feel against my cheek. Clothing hung from every possible angle in the tiny cabin, so I balanced my snowsuit on a nail near the peak of the ceiling. Finding a place where my gloves would dry took some searching and discreet rearranging, but it didn't matter. Jasper was heating up food for anyone who was hungry, and several pairs of eyes followed his every move.

The Montanans had already eaten and were lying in several of the bunks. Karen and I discussed the sleeping options as we wound down and warmed up. There were three people in the double-wide bunk, which was normal. Mushers often dropped all formalities and stretched out alongside complete strangers when the choices were slim. Doug lay in the other bunk and the unoccupied space alongside him seemed luxuriant, if not a bit extravagant. But it just didn't feel right climbing into bed with him. He was not only the reigning champion and perhaps deserving of a certain additional amount of respect, but he had also just announced his plan to marry in Nome at the end of the race and I didn't want rumors getting back to his bride-to-be. The option that remained was the floor.

The floor under the widest bunk looked best for an undisturbed rest, but I cringed at climbing into that darkness. Though it was not spider season, there was a mystery as to what else was under there. I thought of the peanut butter sandwich I had lost, and never found, on the floor of the Trapper Cabin, and now was inclined to crawl under the plank table. Of course, the table would be busy as those now sleeping woke up, and the idea of being a footrest to anyone in this group lacked appeal, but as my belly filled with Jasper's grub, a Thanksgiving-esque kind of euphoria swept over me. I knew I had to lie down. The gods must have taken pity on me though, because at that moment, Doug Swingley stood up to feed his dogs.

Bunks were on a first-come, first-served option at checkpoints. I knew it would take Mr. Swingley at least a half hour to feed his dogs and to waste such a prime sleeping spot for any length of time seemed sinful. Technically, I reasoned, any rights he had on the bunk were actually gone once he got out of bed. With a giddy guilt, I sprawled onto the bunk and, giggling, called out to Karen, "Come on, baby. Come sleep with me!"

We tucked in—head to toe, toe to head—completely filling the space. With Karen's feet somewhere buried in the sleeping bag beneath my head, I tried to reason that this was a more efficient use of space, but before guilt could taint the sweet warmth of my cocoon, I was sound asleep.

An alarm went off deep within the bunk and for a moment I was lost, until I heard Harmony's laughter—it was 5:30 in the morning. I joined the Montanans at the table and waited in line for a plate of Jasper's cooking. Doug had obviously found somewhere else good to sleep because he was quite cheerful. Leaning against the log wall, sipping coffee out of a Styrofoam cup, he described the trail that awaited us.

"The ice on the river will probably be lousy once you leave the woods here. Be careful. The dogs will want to continue down the river, instead of crossing it and entering the woods on the far side. You don't want to go down the river."

"Are you going to bootie?" Even at the early hour Jason was raking the coals for sparks of information.

"Yeah, Terry said the river isn't really glazed over, so it isn't as slick as the Tatina. So I'm going to boot 'em—they need boots going through the tunnels."

Jasper handed me a paper plate with bacon edging a perfectly formed omelet. He was proud of himself, and I was thankful. Working as volunteers together, we hadn't actually gotten along. The combination of two mother hens in one nest had made us strictly rivals. In fact, I had been grateful never to work near him again. However, I had shed the worst of my bad feelings and now felt grateful for his hospitality. Doug refilled his coffee cup and mumbled to himself, though we all instantly knew he meant for us to hear.

"I consider this next stretch to be the worst part of the whole Iditarod Trail."

I set my fork down and closely studied his face. The next thirty miles of trail twisted its way through tight black woods often referred to as the Buffalo Tunnels. Wild bison were often spotted along this part of the trail, and I knew it was rough; I had snow-machined over part of it but . . . worse than the Gorge?

"No way!" I bellowed, immediately regretting the strong tone of my voice. Suddenly I mistrusted the smirk on his face. For years, his confident smile was always reported as a "smirk" by the Alaska newspapers, which unabashedly presented biased stories about the only "Outsider" ever to win the Iditarod. It had almost become a self-serving joke, how much some Alaskans wanted the "guy from Montana" out of the winner's circle. His continued streak of victories seemed to infuriate people. He now looked over at me, and the sincerity in his eyes sent a chill down my spine.

"No, seriously. I think the Buffalo Tunnels and the Post River Glacier are two of the toughest parts of the trail."

Together Karen and I groaned. I knew what lay ahead wasn't easy, but had always figured that if I made it this far—past the Happy River Steps and the Dalzell Gorge—that the insane part was over. More accurately, I'd had never had much faith in making it this far, and thus hadn't seriously considered the 879 miles of trail that remained.

Doug explained the lack of snow that plagued the trail here in the shadow of the Alaska Range—the washboard effect it had—and how it would resemble being on a carnival ride, until we reached the Farewell Lakes area nearly thirty-five miles away. Suddenly I envied Kelly Williams, who had forsaken the comforts of the checkpoint with the plan of camping further down the trail. She had wanted to travel through the rough areas with a tired dog team so they would go slower, and then find a place to pull off, sleeping closer to the area known as the Burn. I had thought she was brave as she explained her plan to me in Rainy Pass, but now I thought she was also wise. I could already imagine the power and speed my fifteen dogs would have after resting more than eleven hours in Rohn. My omelet congealed on my plate, and I forced myself to drink more Tang.

"You'll have time to stop and take off the dogs' booties before you get to the Post Glacier," he continued, obviously enjoying our rapt attention. "And remember. No matter what—go up the right side of the glacier— even if the trail markers point another way."

"Terry told me the same thing," murmured Karen, and I nodded. Jeff had been adamant as well. Somewhere past the crossing of the Post River, the trail climbed a steep glacier. It was very dangerous, though only thirty feet high, and required just minutes—if you were successful. He had explained to me that it was very important for the dogs to stay to the right. The sled needed to hug the cliff so closely on the right side that it scraped the rock wall. From the tone of his voice, I knew he meant for me to remember these instructions. Karen was running dogs for Terry Adkins, a well-respected veteran of the trail, and he had given her the same advice. No matter what, stay right.

I began collecting my gear that lay spread out drying and tried to slip my uneaten omelet into the wood stove without Jasper seeing me, but my David Copperfield move was discovered. Jasper began the nagging that I so clearly remembered from our time together before in this same cabin when he had driven me nearly crazy. I wanted to counter that, no, I wasn't dieting, that no, I didn't mean to be wasteful, but instead quickly escaped outside where the cool air felt clean, and the sweet fragrance of spruce trees made me smile.

I found most of my team sitting upright in their straw beds, looking with interest at the other dogs parked nearby. It was cold; at least −15°F, but beautifully clear. I decided our wake-up snack would be especially filling; I wanted these pups to eat a lot. Maybe if they were full they wouldn't blast me through the Buffalo Tunnels with so much force. Hopefully by our next meal we would be somewhere safe, smooth, and perfectly flat.

I was sweating heavily by the time the team was ready to drive out of the checkpoint. It was nearly eight o'clock, and the Montanans took off just ahead of me. Karen was a little slower getting ready to leave, and I debated waiting for her after she confided in me.

"I am really nervous about this part of the trail."

However, my team was screaming to go and holding them back to wait for her now seemed impossible. Lines would get chewed or something would break. I needed to leave immediately. Feeling guilty, I pulled the hook, leaving Karen behind, shooting through the woods, and then down onto the Kuskokwim River with the full power of a well-rested dog team. Everything happened so quickly I hardly had time to adjust my headlamp before we were skating across the river ice. My hero Salem listened, though, as I calmly repeated "Haw . . . Haw," and we found the entrance into the dark woods on the far side of the skating rink with no problem.

The snow remained blissfully deep for what seemed a long time, and I started to feel a bit smug. I thought of how fun it would be to see buffalo and fantasized that Doug had been just teasing us. The turns were tight, but like a slalom skier, we pivoted left, then right, and then left again with such ease, I felt like I was orchestrating a ballet. It was fun; it was beautiful.

As a volunteer I had spent an afternoon on a snow machine venturing a short way down the trail. I now passed the set of dilapidated buildings I knew to be part of the Pioneer Roadhouse, better known as Frenchy's. This would have been the next roadhouse after Rohn on the Iditarod Trail heading west. I tried to imagine life here after the discovery of gold in 1910. Like a rest stop on the freeway, the roadhouse would have been busy around the clock, servicing dog teams and drivers who carried the mail and supplies in and out of the goldfields.

Would there have been times it felt like—rush hour?

Instead of offering gas, the checkpoints would have dog food and a warm place for the mushers to sleep. Pies would have been popular, as well as daughters and good conversation. The roadhouses would have been a true refuge in this wilderness. Trees now grew out of the cabin roofs, and I wondered about Frenchy. Had he lived out his life here? Ever married? Had he too gone off in search of gold?

Slowly, at first imperceivable, the snow started to thin. The sled started slamming into small trees along the trail, and I began noticing the notches—the healed-over scars left by previous teams. I reminded myself of Jeff's advice, to keep a lookout for these notches, these signs, to see them in advance and be prepared to act. If other people had been running into the same tree for several decades, it likely meant the tilt of the trail or the angle of the turn needed to be carefully negotiated. These weren't the notches that blazed the trails of the Wild West—these notches were made strictly from impact. Many mushers had second sleds waiting for them in Nikolai because this part of the trail was notorious for breaking stanchions and runners. I was concentrating so hard on driving that I was up and nearly onto the Post River Glacier before I saw the crowd.

There seemed to be mushers and dog teams everywhere on the ice, and for a moment, I was totally confused. Jason and Harmony had left Rohn right before me, but I hadn't noticed when Daniel and Doug had taken off and had just assumed they were long gone. They weren't.

I tied my team to a tree in the last bit of woods before the river and then stood by my leaders as I watched the others skating on the glacial ice. I could see a giant frozen waterfall to the right and from there, the river dropped to the left through a boulder field and out of sight through a tangle of rocks and brush. I immediately understood why it was important not to let the team go that way—while the Dalzell Creek had looked narrow and sharp, this frozen waterway looked big and mean, with the ability to swallow the whole team.

The glacier was steep, yet I was comforted that I could at least see the summit, where Doug's sled was snaking just over the pinnacle. Harmony's team must have balked at the climb, veering downstream in the river. It was horrifying to see them straining to continue down into the abyss. She had flipped her sled to add resistance, and she looked tiny trying to crawl with the leaders. Every inch seemed to be painstakingly gained as she tried to grip small brush with one hand, dragging her lead dog with the other.

My dogs were barking and screaming to go, so as soon as I saw Daniel crest the glacier I called out to Salem and he bravely started scrabbling his way across the river. He was doing a great job, resisting the temptation to follow the easier way down the icy trail, and had us nearly across when someone's tug line or harness caught on some brush. The team stopped and the dogs looked back at me.

It was useless, but I shoved my snow hook into a scrap of brush. Calling out, "Easy—easy," I began creeping along the towline to Portland's tug line. It was like ice skating, and several times I fell hard, slamming my knees into the frozen river. I knew if anyone budged before I got finished, the sled would start moving, and the whole team would think it was time to go and start powering forward.

As if on cue, just as I got finished, they surged forward. Luckily, I was able to catch the sled as it went by—except by now Salem's concentration had weakened. He started heading away from the trail and down the river. I started screaming "Gee! Gee!" However, the momentum gained from the slanting ice encouraged speed in everyone. We started quickly sliding down toward what looked to be the Grand Canyon—eons deep. Continuing in that direction would be the end of my Iditarod—I was sure of that—so without hesitating, I flipped the heavy sled, jamming it between two rocks.

Once again, I crawled forward. It was impossible to turn around, and I guided Salem so he was heading back toward the place where incoming trail entered the river. I figured even if we didn't make the haw turn back onto the ice, once I was in the woods again, I could tie off the sled and safely turn the team around.

Back at the sled, I called out and felt a huge surge of pride as Salem crouched and began dragging the team forward in the right direction, taking my commands toward the scratched trail across the ice. We had nearly completed the loop and were just about to the other side of the river—just feet from the dirt bank and a tantalizing reflective marker—when once again someone's line caught on a bit of brush. It brought us to an immediate halt. I leapt from the sled and in seconds had freed the line, but turned in horror at a familiar yelp. Love (in all the wrong places) had happened again. Alto and Shasta were coupled in the middle of the Post Glacier.

I was calm. I did not get mad. I did not cry. For a moment I hesitated, but then methodically went about untangling and petting all the other dogs in the team, knowing it would be at least twenty minutes. Suddenly I heard a cheerful "Hi!" and surprised, turned to see Daniel on foot near my leaders. I could hear his team howling farther up the trail and immediately realized he had come back to help me. It was so dangerous for him to leave his team alone. If they broke a line and took off, the consequences could be horrible. I was eternally grateful, but embarrassed, and waved a hand toward the lovebirds.

"I don't think we're all ready to leave just yet."

He waited with me. Like children whose parents were arguing behind a closed door, his team screamed from up the hill, making it hard for us to converse. In desperation we finally tried something both of us had only heard about. It came from an old musher's bag of tricks. Cold snow, strategically placed, could reduce the swelling of nearly anything, and the two dogs separated. It was too slick for Daniel actually to lead Salem, but by leaping ahead and calling, my good dog followed my new knight up a narrow path that skirted the side of the glacier.

In minutes we reached flat ground where his team was going completely nuts lunging in every direction and hysterically barking. Daniel calmly made sure there were no tangles, and then gave me a little wave before untying the knot that sent him rocketing down the trail. My team took off in hot pursuit and there was no way to slow them down. As I took a sharp breath and looked around, I realized there was something different. The snow had vanished.

CHAPTER 21

A View from the Back

*F*or the next hour or so, it was like life inside a pinball machine. The Gorge was terrifying, but this part of the trail was mean and just plain brutal. The path twisted so tightly through the woods that it seemed impossible not to slam left, slam right, slam left, over and over. When we briefly left the woods, the meadows were no better and often worse, with ornery little tussocks. Just over a foot high, they looked like innocent brush, but actually had the consistency of cement stumps. Ugly protests came from the sled with each impact.

Twice I lost my grip on the handle bow and got separated from the sled. Once, Daniel heard my cry, stopping his team and catching mine as they accordioned into the back of his sled. Again, minutes later, the sled flipped, twisting from my grip. It bounced along the tundra like an Alaskan marionette, but I leapt like Baryshnikov and caught the handle bow as it sailed by midair.

The trail was merciless, serving up complete and total physical abuse. Nearly swept free of snow, the ground felt like asphalt, and my brake was futile on the hard surface. Gone was any semblance of the sled gliding. It simply jumped, slamming from tree to rock to tussock. Now I knew why so many people arrived in Nikolai limping, with broken sleds and smashed hands.

Then it was over.

Doug had foretold this moment in Rohn, but I had only half listened, more worried about the bad than hopeful about the good. He had said that in a single instant you would go from battling the Buffalo Tunnels and afraid for your life—to perfect peace. That the sled would glide again; that in a single, magical moment, all the stress and worries of crossing the Alaska Range would vanish. He had said the hardest part would be over— ahead was just an easy trail to Nome. We had all laughed at this last comment, disbelieving such a thing was possible.

But it was true. In an instant there seemed to be more snow and the sled began to float again. I drew a cautious breath of relief and the thick perfume of evergreens filled me with a gentle peace. We were still in a twisty wood but suddenly it seemed easy, dreamy, as if we were on our way to Grandmother's house. The slightest shift of my weight handily turned the sled, as if simply thinking of it made it so.

We slipped down off a ridge and into a narrow slough. I was now certain that the merciless abuse was over. The light had completely changed. The sunlight had gone from an intense white glare to a soft otherworldly cream that lit the woods like some northern fantasy. Lazy snow crystals dazzled the air as they drifted down from the limbs of fragrant evergreens. There was no doubt in my mind; I had made it through the Buffalo Tunnels.

A series of lakes followed. Gliding along one of these, I received my worst injury of the day when the sled slid sideways into a stump, smashing my knee. For a moment, I saw strobe-illuminated fireworks and felt nauseous, but shortly after that we arrived at Farewell Lake, and the pain dulled when I smelled the sweet wood smoke. At this unofficial, yet sanctioned stop, my friends Shawn and Doro were working in a nearby weather station and had built a fire along the trail. They had made hot water to offer any mushers wanting a break after the grueling ride through the Tunnels.

My intention was to stop only long enough to snack the dogs, but when Cupid aimed his lust-tipped arrow again on Shasta and Alto, I grate- fully used the excuse to vent onto my friends for a few moments. They had both worked at Goose Lake Kennels, so my puppies were delighted to see them; we all beamed at the sound of their familiar voices. Bear Creek cabin made more sense for the long rest, though, because it cut the run more evenly in half, so with regret I finally said good-bye.

At Bear Creek, the others nodded as I pulled in, but continued working on their teams. I quickly set to work myself, laying down a thin layer of straw so my team could snooze in comfort and feeding a snack so they would also nap with full bellies. They were becoming race veterans, serious about making their beds and lying down to rest as soon as possible. Tahoe took great care in arranging her straw, while Hardtack usually just threw himself down somewhere convenient. His course, thick coat allowed him to be comfortable anywhere. Lassen and Bismarck were still the last ones to surrender to sleep, nodding off while sitting upright, then settling down into the straw with their eyes closed. Ice and Latte seemed to enjoy the warmth of each other's bodies, so I made one big pile of straw for the both of them.

Harmony built a fire in the cabin stove, and Doug fussed around looking for ways to make coffee. Soon, the sweet aromas combined, and the crackle of the burning wood beat a cadence that peeled away the memories of the last run. With a steaming cup of coffee in my hands, I found myself lost in laughter. It seemed like so long ago that I had laughed such a deep belly laugh. Harmony took little birdlike bites of food, while Jason discussed the shortfalls of his gear for keeping him warm. My dear Daniel, when he finally came in, sat in a peaceful daze.

Precious Daniel, my knight. At eighteen, the brightness of his cheeks stood out against his pale smooth skin and he looked like a tall six-year-old. He politely turned down my endless offerings of food, chocolate, my firstborn—and smiled shyly at my announcements of love. His kindness in returning for me on the glacier, at such a personal risk, was something I would never forget. Passing him on the trail after the glacier crossing, I had called out to him "I love you, Daniel!"

A bit later I had passed Harmony as well. Her team had balked crossing a small bridge just outside of Farewell Lake, forcing her to take the dogs across one at a time. My team had been power cruising, so we hardly touched the bridge as we flew across, but when I stopped to see if she was all right, she had waved me on. We both had seen Daniel's team coming, so I took off.

Only now did I hear the real story—that indeed, just as I was leaving, Daniel's team was arriving, but there were only twelve dogs, with no sled and no driver! Harmony had leaped out in front of the charging dogs and, hurling her petite weight against all the power of twelve dogs, she had dragged them into the heavy brush along the trail so their tangled lines would hold them. Daniel's towline had broken, so most of the team had raced ahead—in formation—while he, in a panic, desperately pushed his sled on foot. Three dogs remained with him, and together they raced down the trail as fast as he could push them. Daniel traveled for several miles with his miniteam, and I know he must have been pumping madly. Driving a puppy team owned by a past champion myself, I understood the pressures he was under driving Swingley dogs.

The coffee was especially delicious, and I was embarrassed at my own giddy enthusiasm. I realized it was the first cup I had had since before the race had started. I had been so sick to my stomach in the days leading up to the Iditarod that food, never mind coffee, had been nearly impossible to choke down. Now I felt as if a huge weight had been lifted from my body, and I sipped the coffee as if it were the champagne of celebration. I had made it through the Gorge, I had made it through the Buffalo Tunnels—and I knew I would make it through the next 850 miles.

Hours later, just as the sky was turning a brilliant deep red, we left Bear Creek. The trail was flat, straight, and the night's first stars crowded into the sunset. My dogs were eager to get back traveling, and Nikolai awaited us. I hoped my friends from the village would be working the checkpoint, and I was also beginning to look forward to my twenty-four-hour mandatory stop, which I was taking in Takotna. I had never really let myself imagine that long rest, and had avoided fantasizing about the town's reputation for their famous pies—feeling like such arrogance would jinx me. Now I was starting to taste the renowned hospitality.

It was nearly midnight when I got into Nikolai, and felt very relaxed to know my way around the checkpoint. A couple of hours later, after all my chores were done, I stumbled into the school gymnasium. The school's twelve students were having a fund-raiser and making pizza for everybody.

The population of Nikolai was decreasing as more young people moved away, leaving barely enough families with children to support a public school. Balanced on the edge of losing their funding if the numbers decreased any more, the single teacher was a bundle of enthusiasm. The school had cooked up food as a fund-raiser, but was offering to feed the mushers for free.

I joined the folks from Montana, all of whom seemed as dazed as I felt. It had been a beautiful run and the room's warmth was quickly turning us into simpletons. Studying photocopies of the current race updates, Doug kept mumbling names and numbers as he absently took bites of pizza. Finally, he threw the sheets of paper down, laughing.

"This is why I always stayed out front—so I didn't have to bother figuring these things out!"

I didn't care. The front-runners lived in a totally different world than I did. Of course I wanted Jeff and our team to win, but I felt little emotional attachment to them at this point. I wandered back outside to my dogs, and seeing them resting well, made my way to the designated building where mushers slept. I spread my parka and lay down on a dusty floor. Sleep was slow in coming. I was in Nikolai; I had seen so many mushers sleeping just where I lay—curled up with their boots nearby, their hair askew, their socks drying into stiff, unfriendly forms. In the darkness, I muffled my smile into the down of my jacket. I was doing the Iditarod.

CHAPTER 22

Iditarod Pion

*T*wo hours of rest did little to clear my mind, and I wandered around as I prepared to leave. I was shocked to see the time as I finally pulled the hook—somehow I had let an extra hour pass after seeing Harmony and Jason pull out of the checkpoint. The trail crossed the Kuskokwim River, woods, and open country, before dropping down onto the Takotna River—twenty-three miles later. It was sunny, at least 20°F, and the dogs traveled slower and slower as the heat of the day increased. By the time I arrived in McGrath, it was too hot to continue, and I shut the team down to wait out the afternoon.

A woman kindly made me a cheeseburger in the checkpoint and a small boy bounced around the room chanting "G. B. Jones! G. B. Jones!" Would he make it? Secretly I was cheering for this gangly musher with his lopsided grin and deep wrinkles. He was too shy to speak to me, or even remember who I was, because his truck had broken down on the way to this race, while mine matched the sponsored colors of my outfit. I wondered if he had found the time, or energy, to wash the blood off his face from the tree outside of Rainy Pass.

I pulled into Takotna at 7:30 that night, my sixth day on the trail and 436 miles into the Iditarod. The dogs and I were ready for the long break. The heat had zapped what remained of our energy, and I had carried Houston in the sled the entire twenty-three miles from McGrath. Nothing was seriously wrong with him physically, though the cold had irritated a past injury to his testicles. As a young pup he had been frostbitten and the area remained sensitive, so I was constantly on the alert. It was easy to read his expression: "I'm tired, and my balls hurt."

A teenaged girl organized a group of local volunteers to help me park my team. She directed me behind the church into a natural niche of the hillside. From her mannerisms, I took it that she was a pro and completely trusted her commands. It was a perfect place to park the team—out of the wind and in full view of the warm sunshine. Dogs love basking in the sun as much as people do, and it would be great for them to have such a luxurious setting for the layover.

Though most of the dogs were fine, I did have some concerns about Alto, Marco, and of course, Houston, but I knew his problem was a minor physical discomfort. The other two were just not happy, and I decided to make this rest especially nice for them. Their beds got extra straw, and when I massaged their feet and shoulders, I sang old John Denver love songs. Marco wouldn't eat, so at the suggestion of one of the race vets, I begged bacon and eggs off the checkpoint cook. We hand-fed him small bites, and it was enough to whet his appetite.

I had worked with Caroline Griffiths as a volunteer, but it wasn't until now that I fully understood or appreciated her talents. Each year the Iditarod mushers choose a veterinarian who is most helpful and dedicated to the dogs during the race. Caroline had twice won the prestigious Golden Stethoscope Award, and watching her with my own dogs, I realized how much she deserved the praise. This quiet woman had my complete confidence and respect. I hung on every word and beamed at her praise. She said my team looked healthy and especially happy.

Freed from school during the Iditarod, the kids of Takotna diligently worked at the checkpoint. They kept the fires hot under two huge barrels of water next to the church, so we could easily and quickly fix our dogs' meals. They wandered in packs around the dog teams looking for ways to help.

After running daily for nearly a week, I knew it was not a good idea to let the puppies get stiff lying around for twenty-four solid hours. It was against the rules, but I let the kids help me. Because outside assistance is not allowed during the Iditarod, mushers can't receive help feeding their dogs, putting on booties, or hauling water. For the front-runners, any assistance could change the outcome of the race. However, I was running in the back of the pack—and the rules be damned. I decided if the person helping was just over four feet tall, I was willing to risk a penalty.

My new little friends and I took two dogs out at a time—each with two leashes attached to a couple of children. With the stronger boys, I made sure I was on one of the leashes. However, with Lassen, Shasta, and Utah, I let two little girls proudly walk them through the streets of Takotna. We giggled, having a fine time. All the dogs got to stretch and we all enjoyed the young company, taking walks several times during our stay in the village.

Jan, who ran the checkpoint, insisted I tell her when I was ready for a shower. After doing everything I could think of for the dogs, I shyly approached her. Her daughter disappeared, returning with two of the largest, fluffiest towels I could imagine. Her son warmed up his snow machine to drive me over to the Washeteria, and he made sure I had change to run the coin-operated shower. After crashing down the Gorge, losing my team in the Buffalo Tunnels, after slamming my knee into a tree—my eyes finally overfilled with tears.

This had been one of my many fears of running the Iditarod—that I would embarrass myself by crying when something went wrong—and so far, I'd kept it together. Yet at the sight of those towels, and the kindness in those strangers' faces, it was everything I could do not to completely break down.

Since my dogs were parked next to the church, it was a great place for me to relax as well. I hauled in my personal gear, swearing to organize and reduce what I was carrying, and spread it out along several pews. I was alone when I took off my baseball cap and realized what was embroidered on the front of it.

At Finger Lake, I had walked past Joe Runyan whose book on sled dogs I had been carefully studying all winter. He was a major writer covering the race and was often at the checkpoints. He had nodded his head, and in his Midwestern-aw-shucks accent, said, "Good luck, champ."

I had simply waved and kept walking, assuming he was just being nice to a rookie. Now, in mock horror, I sat on the chapel pew, laughing at the hat I held in my hands. At the start of the race, I had simply grabbed a baseball hat from the dog truck, never looking at the logo. This had been a mistake. Obviously, it was one of Jeff's. Emblazoned across the front, in bold letters, it declared: "IDITAROD CHAMPION."

I had been wearing it for more than half the race—me, a measly rookie! What in the world had Joe Runyan thought of my highfalutin attire? I set it down and stretched luxuriously out on the floor of the main chapel. It was a quiet and peaceful place to sleep, though for a while I had a hard time stifling the giggles. Later, I found a marker pen and carefully scratched out half the letters, leaving a more suitable label: "IDITAROD PION."

All my friends from Montana had done their twenty-four-hour layovers in McGrath. It was good to see their dog teams arriving the next afternoon. Jason, Harmony, and Daniel stayed just five hours and then pulled out like a pack of wild horses. Doug left at 8:09 P.M., and since my time was up just three minutes later, I stood poised and ready to chase.

I knew I just had puppies. I knew Doug Swingley was driving his championship team. But I also knew it was just thirty-eight miles to Ophir and my dogs were rested and screaming to go down the trail. I decided it would be fun to push them a little—to chase Doug.

Off we shot. Jeff had told me this would be one of my best runs of the entire Iditarod. The trail was good, the dogs would be full of magic after their long rest and, personally, I would feel great after sleeping and eating well. I had been looking forward to it—and now with the extra delight in chasing a champion, I put my head down and pumped with all my might. The sled charged forward as if it were autonomous. Several of the dogs looked back toward me and grinned. We were a team!

At the edge of the village, the road seemed to split. My lead dogs, Salem and Bismarck, dove confidently to the left and with only the slightest, tiniest of doubts, I loosened the reins and let 'em roll. We were immediately soaring, and the night sky was so clear the stars crowded the darkness. I gazed down at the team of sled dogs in front of me and once again felt the shock of realizing where I was, and what I was doing. I was driving sled dogs across the Alaskan wilderness by myself. Just a couple of years ago this would have seemed as unlikely to me as singing on Broadway.

I uttered a cry of happiness that hit the team like a mounting wave coming toward the beach. We swept forward, hurling through the night with images of Santa's sleigh rising into flight—making anything seem possible.

CHAPTER 23

Cold, Dark Trails to Ophir

*A*t first I ignored the fact that I saw no trail markers. The Iditarod followed a road between Takotna and Ophir, and obviously there would be only one road this deep within the Interior. Soon a bridge appeared and I remembered vaguely the boss explaining something about a slat bridge. I whooped the dogs up so the boys up front wouldn't hesitate, and they took the bridge like professionals, literally dancing across the widely spaced boards. I nervously looked at the ice far below and only felt confident knowing nearly fifty other teams had already crossed the bridge safely. The steep drop on the other side rudely jolted the sled. The creepy sound of the impact seemed to hang in the air as it reverberated in the tunnel of trees.

It got darker and much colder. I reached up to touch my headlamp—was the battery already going dead? Should I pull out my big parka? The sweat I had produced from chasing Doug began to feel clammy against my skin. It took a great effort to help push the sled. I obsessively swept my headlamp back and forth on every other swing of my leg, but no matter how hard I looked, there was no sign that anyone else had recently traveled here.

Where were the damn trail markers? The thin pieces of wooden lathe were supposed to help guide me.

On and on we went. My thoughts strayed to my parents' divorce twenty years earlier, and the family decorations my mother still bravely put out each year. I pictured David alone in Uganik looking out at the rain and my father telling me he had diabetes. I even sadly wondered where the family poodle had been buried while I was away at college. I saw no trail markers and I knew there was no way yet for me to turn this dog team around. My legs felt like dead weight. I was cold but didn't have the energy to put on more clothes. I had fallen off Takotna's euphoric edge.

The thin layer of snow made the prospect of turning my enthusiastic team around seem impossible. If I was not on the trail, I needed to find a place to tie off the sled while I rotated the dogs. If indeed I was lost.

But I am on the road! And there was the bridge! I can't start getting paranoid now!

The road ended at a cluster of buildings illuminated by an eerie light. With certainty, I knew I had done something terribly wrong. The dogs charged into the lit parking lot, and I scratched the brake to slow them as much as possible. It had no effect; the sled veered sideways, and as I passed a tall metal sign, I threw my snow hook like a lasso, the sharp crack of metal-to-metal sounding like an inner-city gunshot.

Where in the hell was I?

The dogs went insane, obviously as surprised as I at the scene. Their frenzied lunging made the sled buck on its tether, threatening to dislodge the snow hook or worse, snap the line. If they left me now there was no telling where in the world they would end up: Timbuktu, Russia, Manhattan.

"Hello! Hello!" Huge generators muffled my voice, and I was surprised how small I sounded—that couldn't possibly be me speaking.

"Oh—help! Help! Is anyone here?"

It was now snowing lightly. The dogs' leaping left scuff marks on the asphalt. I couldn't leave the sled to turn them around and knew after a few moments of calling commands that they wouldn't listen to me. My voice would seem like I was just joining them in their barking. Suddenly a door opened to the closest building, and an old man shuffled out. Shielding his eyes from the falling snow, he stared out across the lot at me.

"Hello—hello," I cried out to him and he shuffled slightly closer. My voice had a pitiful whine to it. "I think I may be lost!"

I was shocked to see that he was wearing shorts, and for a moment we simply stared at each other. The dogs danced like marionettes on their strings in front of me, and somebody's papaw was wearing shorts in a snowstorm. It was like an Alaskan Fellini movie. I was confused and desperate, and I really had to question whether this was all part of some strange dream.

Could it be possible I was still up in Denali and this was another one of my prerace nightmares? Between the dogs screaming and the generator, the noise was deafening. The old man held a hand up to his ear, scooting even closer. I glanced at my team, but they certainly seemed real.

Turning back to the man I shouted above the din of their barking. "I think I'm lost!" The dogs were lunging in every direction—first toward him and then away, barking madly. Wryly I wondered if they would ever go hoarse.

He shuffled closer and then, almost politely, shouted back at me. "Where are you going?"

And with these words I knew my worst fears were true.

I was supposed to be on the Iditarod Trail. Some fifty other mushers had already gone ahead of me on their way to Nome. If this man did not immediately know where I was going with fifteen screaming sled dogs in the middle of the night—then I was lost. Really lost.

For a second I stared at him, hoping he was kidding, but there was nothing joking about his expression. He was waiting for my decision. I caught sight of Salem, between his blind lunges, looking back at me as well. This sinking ship was mine alone to save. I reached up to straighten my headlamp and then gripped the handle bow.

"I gotta turn the team around. Can you grab my leaders and pull them over there?"

I hated asking. He looked so old, and he must have been cold. He calmly waved, though, and edged bravely up to Salem and Bismarck. I was surprised how easily they began to turn, and was briefly feeling hopeful— when suddenly I saw a flash of light and *The Pet* came into view. My dogs went berserk.

There is something about pet dogs that drives sled dogs crazy.

They nearly knocked the old guy over as they leapt in the wrong direction, ripping free from his grip, lunging and baying at the top of their voices. The snow hook clattered against the metal post that shuddered with each impact, the line attaching us to it looking dangerously more fragile by the moment. I screamed from the sled, but felt helpless. If I left the sled, and something went wrong—things would get much worse.

The old man shuffled over to *The Pet* and tried waving him off. Each time he turned his back to return to my team, the dog came forward, inciting complete chaos and frenzy in my dogs. I had only seen such complete madness with stray pets. It was as if sled dogs knew these critters were of a different class, not working class. My sweet puppies wanted to shred him to pieces.

Bravely the guy grabbed the leaders, though twice more they knocked him down. I was just about to call him off—though I couldn't imagine what I would do without his help—when the door opened again. An old woman stepped out of the building in her night robe. She quickly pushed *The Pet* inside and then stood there clutching herself. It must have been at least −10°F, but she looked calmly at the scene before her. I imagined she smelled like my grandmother, and knew exactly how my cheek would feel tucked against her flannel nightgown.

"I think I made a really, really big mistake," I cried out gloomily.

With all the commotion ricocheting around us, she looked at me with incredible kindness, an incredible sense of calm. Her words were disturbing, yet her comforting tone is what I wanted to hear most.

"Oh, honey, you're going to be all right." She covered her ear closest to the barking madness. "It's only ten miles back to Takotna!"

With a heavy heart I retraced the long miles back to Takotna. I slowed the team down to a crawl as we crossed the bridge, now really seeing how widely spaced the boards were, how easily a dog could catch and break its leg. The dogs were tired and I could barely keep my eyes open from depression. I wanted to curl into a fetal position and wake up anywhere else.

At the crossroads to the village I only hesitated in my mind. I could go back to Jan and get another shower and I'd probably find a willing kid to help me park my team, but actually I knew there was no choice. I called "Haw!" with all my might and we turned west into the dark night for the long trudge to Ophir.

CHAPTER 24

Takotna to Cripple—the Long Way

*I*t was 10:30 at night, and I was cold and tired. After two and a half hours on the trail from Takotna, I was back where I'd started—except now my team had lost their sparkle. We slowly trudged up the first hill. I tried pumping as much as possible, but my heart wasn't into it. I sang out to the dogs, but my tunes fell on deaf ears. Gently falling snow obscured anything but their backsides and the reflective markers I obsessively followed. By the time I arrived in Ophir, a twenty-five-mile run had turned into a fifty-miler. My snowsuit felt like an armor of ice, and I was totally disgusted. What should have been one of the most enjoyable runs of the race had turned into an embarrassment that had not only cost me more than two hours of time, but that had concerned race officials calling back to Takotna looking for me. My mistake was not simply a private matter between me and my team; it had already been broadcast up and down the trail.

I should have loved being in Ophir. In 1907, more than a thousand people lived here chasing the elusive dream of gold. The log cabin I entered had been a checkpoint in every Iditarod for thirty years and with a roaring fire, hot coffee, and good company, would have been my idea of heaven—but it was almost three in the morning when I stepped through the door. I started looking for a place to rest, and I never really found it.

Everything was wet—my snowsuit, *anorak*, my socks—even my beaver hat was soaked with sweat and condensation. The log cabin was jam-packed with mushers, veterinarians, and race judges. Three gruff old men sat regally in the choicest spot nearest the warmth of the woodstove. They were gold miners, and this was their cabin. They grunted when I asked about hot water to drink and hanging up some of my clothes. One guy begrudgingly shifted in his chair to allow me to lean past and hang my *anorak*, but then groaned loudly when it barely brushed his arm. I was cold and hungry, but wanted more just to give up on this long night. My back hurt, and painfully I lowered myself onto the plank floor next to a sleeping form I recognized as Karen's.

By the time I lay down, one of the old guys had unrolled a wide foam pad and luxuriously spread out. The rest of us were crammed on the floor like a package of hotdogs. A murderous cold rose from the floorboards, and every time the door to the cabin opened, an evil cloud of cold fog rolled into the room, looming under the low ceiling. After awhile, I climbed back into my wet snowsuit, but it had stiffened and offered no comfort.

The cold from the floor was killing me. I had dull images of the gray chill slowly reaching every bone and muscle fiber in my body, frosting, congealing my blood. Eventually, very slowly, I began inching, a toe, a foot, the tip of my shoulder, an edge of a buttock, then half my butt—onto my neighbor's foam pad. Every millimeter gained brought immense relief, and fear encouraged patience. Finally I heard an angry grunt.

"Get off my bed!" the old guy hissed at me, roughly shoving my bony hip. "And stay off!"

He probably outweighed me by a hundred and fifty pounds; four of us could have fit on his damned pad. I turned away, onto my side, slipping an arm out of my sleeve and tried to balance on the minimal padding. The minutes crept by. Twice I stood up to rub feeling into my numb shoulder and hip. At some point, the old man got up and seeing me sitting upright once again hissed at me. "And don't you dare touch my bed!"

I didn't understand why he needed to be so mean. I decided it was a good thing for the entire universe that he lived out here in the middle of friggin' nowhere. I was sick of him and sick of the whole damned race. I lay back down on the floor and, for the rest of the night, the foam pad lay empty beside me, soft and warm. All I needed in the whole world.

I sensed it was a mistake, but I cut the dogs' rest the next morning so I could chase the Montanans. I knew it was a risk, but hearing Harmony's laughter made the trials less forbidding. Daniel's quiet demeanor and obsessive care for his puppies made him a good role model, and Jason was always willing to offer advice. It was fun to travel with them. And then there was Doug.

For years, I had heard and been around enough of Doug Swingley to know I had no interest in knowing him better. Cocky and overconfident, Doug of the Media might be a phenomenal dog breeder and musher, but that did not impress me. Most of my judgments of people came from how they handled old people, strangers, and animals. He had always failed miserably in the stranger department.

However, this man, this year, was different. I enjoyed running with him. He was patient with the children in the checkpoints, kind to their parents. He shared hints and stories of the trail without a trace of the arrogance I had seen before. I had begun to realize that perhaps the line was blurred between confidence and arrogance, and perhaps it was one that could be easily, and accidentally, crossed. After working for someone who was a celebrity as well, I also realized how much stretch could exist between public opinion and the truth. I was enjoying the surprise of actually liking the guy from Montana that so many Alaskans had pretended to hate. He was pleasant to be around; besides, I thought of it as traveling with an Olympic coach.

Therefore, I left Ophir after resting the dogs just six hours—chasing Harmony in the early light, grateful to be away from the oppressive ghost town full of grumpy old men. Later, somewhere in the flats, halfway to Cripple, I joined the others resting at the edge of a wood through the day's heat. Karen caught up with us there. Daniel and I talked about our puppies; Karen shared caffeinated drinks and funny stories about her lead dog, Pig. Harmony laughed, and Jason questioned me about life at Goose

Lake Kennels. I left in the early afternoon sometime between Karen and Doug, though I never saw either again before arriving in Cripple, several gray hairs later.

There are sixty miles between Ophir and Cripple. After a nice long afternoon rest, I figured on arriving at the tent checkpoint in the early evening. The sun was setting orange as I entered a small hilly area, and several times, I felt like I must have taken a detour, though I always rejoined what felt like the main Iditarod Trail. I arrived at a confusing cluster of reflective stakes as a black pitch began edging the twilight out of the sky. I chose to go right, and for a few moments worried, but shortly a reflective marker flashed from the tree trunk and we happily continued on down the trail.

I should have been in Cripple by 8:00, or 8:30—or maybe somewhere after 9:00 if my breaks had been longer than I thought. By ten o'clock, I was having the familiar sticky hot flashes I felt on the first trail out of Takotna and my stomach was burning. I was still following widely spaced race stakes, but there were no tracks on the trail ahead of me. Although the blowing wind would quickly erase the trail, I somehow felt there should be some kind of sign that the Montanans had recently passed. Once again worry sucked the energy out of my limbs and weighed my heart with guilt. What had I done wrong this time? But there were trail markers! What was going on? When eleven o'clock came, I finally stopped the team. I would wait for Karen—this was getting too weird. At this point we should have arrived at the checkpoint.

By midnight, I was scared. *Where in the hell was I now? Where was Karen?* She should have left the afternoon rest stop soon after me; she should have been just behind me. I had stopped right next to a trail marker to reassure myself, but now it looked old and weather-beaten. Had I somehow gotten on an old Iditarod Trail? One no longer used—that did not go to any checkpoint at all?

Set up in a different spot every year, placement of the Cripple checkpoint totally depends on how the Yukon River has frozen. The old gold-mining town long ago melted back into the wilderness, so the checkpoint is simply located on the most conducive spot to land a ski plane in the general area. Arctic tents were set up to house the checkers and offer the mushers respite from the infamous deep cold of the area, but tents were still tents, no matter what the die-hard outdoor enthusiasts said.

Still, I dreamed of these structures as I sat next to Lassen, waiting for the warm glow of Karen's headlamp to peek through the woods. Sometimes a random snowflake would catch a reflection and my heart would soar—thinking how good it would be to see her wonderful smile— to hear her Midwestern drawl. She was from Indiana; she knew about basketball and fried chicken. She knew about Jell-O salad and tiny great-aunts with patent leather shoes and matching purses. Without ever asking, I knew she understood about homecoming queens and sororities.

But she never did show up; somehow I was lost again. This time though, no kindly couple was going to offer me gentle words of encour-agement. Quite literally I was in the middle of nowhere. My snowsuit felt like a lead weight; even lifting my arms to adjust my headlamp took considerable effort. I was exhausted and had already begun to hallucinate during the last hour of traveling, seeing the small people of the woods, hearing low-flying airplanes in the middle of the night. Even my dogs were weary; they had begun to flag in the last hour. I knew if I tried to turn them around now and stumble back down the trail to God knows where, they would end up depressed as well.

I decided to stay put until first light and painfully organized to spend the rest of the night waiting. I had some Red Robin burgers, which I broke into little portions so each dog would at least get a taste. I was severely dehydrated, but had run out of Heet to melt snow. If I grew too cold, I knew I could make a fire, but for the time being decided to save my energy. I was really tired and needed to rest so I could think clearly and steer my dogs back out of this mess. I pulled out my sleeping bag and the biggest chemical heat pad I had tucked away for emergencies. I found a dog blanket and laid it out on the ground. I put my parka on over my suit and found my beaver hat. I pulled out my over-mitts so my clenched fists could stay warmer and leaned against the sled.

The northern lights flickered across the black sky in rolling sheets of color, gently illuminating my sleeping team. Occasionally there was a crackle and even shadows from the heavenly show. I stared despondently into the dark forest around me, refusing to look up. I didn't admire my pups and I didn't gaze in wonder at the lights. I didn't deserve any of them.

Mark Nordman was the Iditarod Race Marshal. During the heat of the race, his job was to keep things flowing as smoothly as possible. There were race judges at each of the checkpoints, but the final say on procedures or rules was ultimately up to him. He was a mild-mannered man with a full beard and laugh lines surrounding his eyes. He had the gentle voice of a priest. He was a friend, and through the years, we had discussed lives and births, deaths and marriages. I knew he had been especially pleased to see me work my way from volunteer to handler to musher, and I knew withdrawing me from the race would be especially hard on him.

When a musher falls too far behind everyone else in the race, something has to be done. There is an unwritten time span allowed, but the reality is that the checkpoints must be closed in a timely manner. With a staff of volunteers in the villages, in the air, and covering the trail on snow machines—at some point it needs to be over, things need to wrap up.

For a while, there was a rule that in order to stay in the race someone in the back of the pack needed to be within a certain number of days behind the front-runners, but this often seemed unfair. The new rule was more vague, stating a musher needed to be "competitive" and relied more on individual circumstances than a blanket rule. Most people realized when they had fallen too far behind everyone else and gracefully scratched themselves from the race. It was always a terribly difficult decision, hard on everyone, but it was even harder to be forced to withdraw. If a musher did not realize how far behind he or she was—then the Race Marshal flew in.

Tired and depressed, I convinced myself I was lost in a maze of trails somewhere near the Yukon River. I imagined the search planes would come the next day, and then the helicopters. Obviously, I was nowhere near where a plane could land. Mark was a friend. I knew this would make it even harder on both of us. I imagined the kind gestures as he quietly told me I was now so far behind the rest of the pack that I would have to withdraw. I had been warned that some of the days on the Iditarod Trail would be some of the best, and worst, of my life. Being lost was certainly not the worst, but was certainly one of the most depressing.

I dozed and twice packed up the sled to go, but then had second thoughts. The puppies needed to feel good when the challenges of tomorrow came. I just couldn't let myself go floundering in the woods with them tired. I was an educator, a coach, and my job was to encourage them, to teach them, to guide them through this difficult journey and have them finish with positive feelings. If I was withdrawn, there was no reason they should know defeat.

By the gray light of morning, I had turned the team around and was moving. The trail was completely swept free of my tracks; I had to keep turning my head to look backward to see the trail reflectors on the trees. After a couple hours, I came to the fork in the trail and could see how in the morning light the markers indicated a left turn, and not a right, like the one I had taken. A few moments later, I arrived at the Cripple checkpoint. It was 7:30 A.M.

The Montanans came out of the shelter tent looking well rested, but relieved to see me. Karen had arrived at nine o'clock last night, which had made it clear there was a problem with my progress.

Jason was incredulous. "Where have you been?" Harmony gave me a long hug and laughed nervously. "I bet you had a long night?"

Doug didn't make a single comment, didn't ask a single question. After a silent hug, he gave me the hand towel he had in his hand. I had indicated "towel envy" several times in the past few days, a good thing to wipe your hands on between putting ointment on the dog's feet and eating finger foods. Both Daniel and Doug had sent fresh ones out in their drop bags, so were constantly sending the dirty ones home. I had jokingly begged for an old one.

The race officials had been on alert, waiting for daylight to call in planes. Since Cripple was not a village, and no one lived within sixty miles, there were no snow machines to borrow. The search would have been conducted by air—just as I had had nightmares about in the night. But, typical for an exhausted mind, my perceptions had been off. There was no talk of withdrawing me from the race. There were still plenty of people behind me. My race was far from over.

CHAPTER 25

Among the Best

I stayed in Cripple just two and a half hours, long enough to feed the dogs a proper meal and let them digest awhile before going on. I left at 10:00 with Devon Currier departing a half hour after me. He was on his second attempt at finishing the Iditarod and had a quiet confidence I liked. Karen followed, traveling with a mixture of rookies and veterans that made up the back of the pack.

The volunteers were so friendly in Cripple that I hated to leave, but knowing the hot sun would soon shut me down, I hurried farther down the trail. From Don Bowers's "Trail Notes," I knew there was an old mining road the last fifty miles into Ruby, and I vaguely pinpointed the bridge at Sulatna Crossing as a goal to reach before resting. Once again I had hopes that even though the road was not maintained, I wouldn't get lost out of Poorman.

The trail twisted through the Ruby Hills, and though no one currently lived anywhere nearby, there were frequent signs of the mining that occupied the district in the early part of the century. I regretfully passed collapsed cabins and rusting pieces of steel. It seemed criminal to be in a race, neglecting all this history.

As it got warmer, the dogs started slowing, and I began looking for a good spot in the trail for a break. I was not seeing signs of my bridge. With so many teams behind me, I needed a place to pull off so they could easily pass. I also hoped for a place inviting enough that would encourage Karen to stop as well. I was still shook up from spending the night lost, and for the first time really wanted some company.

A wide curve with perfect exposure to the afternoon presented itself, and as soon as I stopped the team, they were digging nests in the snow. I quickly snacked the dogs so they would sleep digesting calories. Karen and Sandy McKee, another rookie, soon joined me, and we had a pleasant afternoon, filled with girl talk and dog talk.

From Poorman through Sulatna and Long, the road to Ruby winds through lonely wilderness across countless creeks and gulches. Though closed in the winter to anything but dog teams and snow machines, it had almost an urban feel—but in a creepy manner. The abandoned town of Long was far too modern to be so dark and empty of life, and I hurried the dogs down the trail. The bustling activity of 1911 was shadowed now in the summer, when the road was open and small mining ventures operated nearby—but in March, the buildings were mostly buried in snow, and the road signs peered out of tall drifts. It felt like the movie set of a seventies film I had seen on a nuclear holocaust.

Mean, icy patches of overflow frequently blocked the trail. Under insulated layers of ice, water continues to flow all winter in northern regions. Heavy snowfall will push down on the ice though, forcing the warmer water to the surface through cracks. It eventually solidifies, like lava, into a layered dome of ice. These areas are either still forming, thus wet and slushy, or rock hard, tilted like a sinking boat and slick as hell. I tensely balanced the sled on the uphill runner for long, exhausting periods. It took all my strength with the heavy sled, but I was glad I had been able to practice the move on the Horse Trail. I had been obsessive about it—even carrying extra weight at times just to practice on that fifty-foot piece of slanting trail. More than once I had not thrown my own weight correctly, or misplaced a foot and had tipped the sled over, packing snow into my eyes so hard I couldn't see, and jamming ice crystals up my nose. Eventually I had improved, and for a moment now I wondered where my coach was. *How was the boss holding up? Which of the dogs were turning into superstars?*

I had spent so much time with every dog on his team; I knew each one of them well. So many training runs to Gold King and on the Denali Highway—hours of massage and late nights packing meals for the camping trips. They should be on the coast by now, and I hoped the wind was kind and they were charging. I also hoped that Jeff was happy with their position, whatever it was.

Periodically I waited for Karen, Sandy, and Devon, finding great comfort in seeing their headlamps. This really felt like a desolate part of Alaska, and I had no desire to be alone in it. Perhaps it was the hour, or perhaps the sheer number of abandoned buildings and frozen remnants of human activity, but time crept. The place was just too spooky to enjoy the trail.

Finally, rounding a turn, the lights of Ruby came as a huge relief. Here the road had been plowed free of most of its snow, so suddenly we were flying down a long hill. I did not have the least ability to slow the team down. They could smell the wood smoke, and knew what was coming. They started bounding with a glee I hadn't seen for awhile. I was exhausted from wrestling the sled over the nasty ice, but the lights of this famous village sparkled so invitingly, and with the dogs' renewed enthusiasm, I sailed into the checkpoint out of breath and smiling. It was nearly 12:30 at night. A lifetime had passed since leaving Ophir.

Locals scurried about getting the drop bags and straw for the dogs. The checkpoint had two long tables filled to overflowing with the countless food dishes of a potluck supper. It was a feast, hosted by the people of Ruby. The faceless kindness deeply touched me. As these days passed, either the kindness of strangers was increasing, or I was simply seeing more of the depth of the Iditarod than I had ever imagined. A young man with a sweet Athabascan accent gave me words of encouragement as I boiled water for my dogs, a deep fatigue slowing my speech. I so appreci- ated his company and words that I offered him granola bars and candy to keep talking.

The air in the log church where the mushers bedded down was sticky with perspiration and heat. Everybody was soaked from the countless crossings of overflow, and gear hung from every possible point. It had been an exhausting run, and I gratefully sank into my sleeping bag, the carpet as spongy as the softest feather bed I could imagine. Just before falling asleep, I heard Karen mumbling to no one in particular.

"That was the eeriest place I think I have ever been. It's good to be here." Muffled agreement came from around the room. The saving grace to the Poorman Road was the jewel of the Yukon: the village of Ruby.

I headed back down onto the Yukon River late the next morning. Devon had already gone after resting his dogs eight hours, and Ken Chase, a Native man from the village of Anvik, left just ahead of me. The day was overcast and I had decided to risk letting the dogs rest an hour longer. The run that followed was worth the wait.

The dogs flew to Galena. The dreaded monotony of the Yukon River was a wonderful relief for both the dogs and me, giving us wings. There were happy yelps as the pups raced along, and I joined—serenading them with John Denver and old Girl Scout songs. When I stopped to hand out snacks, everyone wagged their tails and soon barked to go on.

Let's go! Let's go!

The checkpoint at Galena perched on the edge of the river, and a lively group of local women chatted with me as I did my chores. The laughter came so easily, the humor so gentle and caring, that immediately I knew this had to be a village with a strong community of women. They were bright, artistic, and likely pretty tough, despite the fancy fringe and ribbons decorating their parkas.

I quickly fed the dogs, eager to join everyone else in the crowded checkpoint. It was another lively group, and I was thrilled to hear my team had done the run faster than anyone else yet in the race—even the champion team of Doug Swingley, who had rested longer at Ruby! It had taken us just four hours and forty minutes to do the fifty-two miles from Ruby.

Jeff's daughters had sent me a bag of goodies to the checkpoint, and I shared the edible tidbits, giving away the toys to the children. It felt like a

Christmas party, and I hated to take a nap when so many wonderful people were around, but finally I succumbed to exhaustion and lay down in a room in the back of the building.

Galena to Nulato was another fifty-two miles. I pulled out just as the sun was setting in hopes of arriving before too terribly late. Since my last run had been so spectacular, I had fantasies of the next miles going quickly, perhaps catching back up with some of the Montanans and making up for the time I had lost between Takotna and Cripple. We sailed down onto the river with all the best intentions.

The snow cover on the river thickened to the consistency of deep, loose sand, and our winter dance turned to a tedious trudge. As the beam of my headlamp gradually faded onto the flats of the wide Yukon River, my world became the sugary snow and marching backsides of my dogs. I knew they loathed it as much as I did.

During the previous summer I had tried memorizing distances between checkpoints and had put flashcards all around my fish camp. Looking for a diversion, my crewmember Josh had taken up the game, and though the Iditarod Trail was as foreign to him as dining on caviar in Paris, he dutifully studied. At any time, I could ask him.

"Josh, how far between Galena and Nulato?"

"Fifty-two miles."

"How long will it take with a fast dog team?"

"Galena to Nulato should take four hours."

"How long will it take with a slow dog team?"

"Five and a half hours." He spoke in a robot tone as he pulled the salmon out of the net and tossed them into bins in the boat. How painfully accurate was his guess on a slow dog team! The pace leadened our limbs, completely depressing all of us. How much further to Nome I thought grimly—350 more miles, and I had been on the trail more than ten days.

I smelled smoke and guessed we were passing the village of Koyokuk in the darkness, past Bishop's Rock and the possibilities of nasty winds that frequently boiled around it, but the night was a flat and heavy calm.

I couldn't imagine another challenge for my pups, but briefly dreamed that even a wind would be salvation from the endless trudge.

I arrived in Nulato exhausted, though briefly cheered by the large, kind men tending a fire with water for the dogs. The Natives of Nulato were Athabascan, tall with deep voices. They joked with me as I wearily began my chores—though it was nearly three in the morning, and I guessed they hadn't been to bed yet either. I had to work hard to stay focused, to get through my chores so I could lie down. I kept resisting the urge to curl up in the straw with the puppies—they looked so sweet and comfortable. Finally, when at last I did lay my head down, it was on some hard, narrow bleachers in the school gym. Nothing had ever felt softer.

One of my little girls had a problem I couldn't figure out. Utah was vaguely lame, but neither the vet nor I could find a specific sore area. After walking her with a leash around the village to see if I could loosen her up, I decided to drop her. She was the sweetest kisser in the whole kennel and a steady puller, though she only weighed forty pounds. Utah was usually a happy girl and I hated leaving her behind, though I knew Tahoe would be thrilled.

Tahoe and Utah, for no apparent reason, had always hated each other with a deathly passion. They were two dainty little girls, and yet when they came within sight of one another, both became tigers, clawing to get close and rip the throat out of the other. They were the only two dogs in the entire kennel I had refused to let run free for even the briefest moment, because they would immediately search the other out. Once after spending the night with me, cuddling and playing for hours on the carpet, Tahoe had slipped from my grip as I was leaving the cabin. I had flown after her knowing the next minutes could affect my Iditarod team. Just as I feared, she had run straight to Utah's house, grabbed the smaller dog by the neck, and was shaking with all her might when I arrived. I grabbed Utah and wrapped my arms around her for the next long minutes, blocking the killer dives of Tahoe. I held no angel in my arms, though, and the moment I released my grip, she flew with teeth bared.

Still I hated to leave her. For such a small dog, she had contributed a great deal to our trip, but when the vet started to take her, I had to laugh. Tahoe turned her head away with an exaggerated look of disgust—exactly like a triumphant, bratty teenager.

After we rested for six hours, we once again began the trudge down the Yukon River. This time, the heat and slow trail combined to slow us to an absolute crawl. After several mind-numbing hours, I finally stopped the team midafternoon. I couldn't handle it; the forty-two miles was taking forever, and we were just going too damned slow. Looking at my watch, I decided to give the dogs a three-hour siesta. I unpacked a dog blanket to sit on and willed myself to remain still. I wasn't sleepy and it took all my self-control to stay put, but the dogs napped peacefully in the warm sunshine. I ate granola bars and stared at the sky. Beyond the banks of the river, the land rose a few feet and then leveled off forever flat. I had a hard time believing they called this place Alaska.

CHAPTER 26

The Wonder of Fine Company

*W*hen most of the world thinks of sled dogs, they picture Siberian huskies. The blue-eyed furry creatures have the solid build and thick coat that appeals to the Jack London image we all grew up loving. Leonhard Seppala, the famous Nome musher who owned Balto and Togo, made famous by the Serum Run of 1925, did indeed race Siberians. For years, they were the fastest dogs of the North, but their position in modern-day dog racing has changed. Many of the Alaskan huskies now have so much hound and other breeds mixed into the bloodlines that no one outside the sport would guess that such small, short-haired animals could be champion long-distance sled dogs. Siberians were loveable, like big teddy bears—mellow and steady, and often very slow. *Slow-beriuns* was a term I had often heard.

When I shut down the team on the Yukon, a team of Siberians passed me. I had to laugh, because I did not want to cry. Here I was driving a team of dogs I hoped would be Iditarod champions—dogs whose bloodlines could be traced to some of the fastest long-distance sled dogs in the world—and I was passed by Siberians! Nikolai Ettyne briefly stopped and agreed, yes, it was hot, but his team was moving fine. He wanted to continue just a bit farther down the trail. They seemed happy enough as they pulled away, like goofy stuffed animals, but they were moving along quite cheerfully. I looked at my sleeping babies and hoped I was not being overly cautious.

When my watch finally allowed me to wake them up, I sang songs and did little dances in front of the team. I called out their favorite nicknames and raised my arms as I twirled in circles. They were groggy, but my antics had to make them laugh. I saw the slight movement of tails, and when several started barking to go, I quickly pulled the snow hook with a rebel yell. I was grateful no one else was around. I certainly didn't want anyone to catch my theatrics.

In seconds we went from first to fifth gear. We rounded the first bend on that wide Yukon River like the homestretch of the Kentucky Derby—galloping with our tails held high. The wind felt good on my cheeks and I whooped with delight feeling the happy surge of the team. What a wonderful day to be running! It was spring! Life was grand!

Then, to my complete surprise and dismay, I spotted buildings.

A village stretched along the banks of the river just ahead of us. The sunlight glinting off the roofs of several cabins winked from a short distance, I could hear the whine of four-wheelers racing along the streets, and instinctively I cried out. I knew there was only one explanation. I had shut down the dogs just fifteen minutes too early! I had arrived at Kaltag, the next checkpoint.

The race officials met me coming into the village with huge grins and looks of admiration. My guys had looked absolutely fantastic coming down the Yukon River! They had called people to come watch—to see this Iditarod team with wings nearly eight hundred miles into the race!

What a beautiful sight. Now these were some great dogs!

A small crowd gathered, chattering excitedly about the fantastic performance of my team. Many called out congratulations. In this country, the Athabascans had honored fast sled dogs for hundreds of years. They stood back respectfully to allow me room to work. It was flattering to be treated like the celebrity front-runners, and I tried to gracefully accept the compliments. But to myself I thought wryly, of course they looked great, this was probably the first team that entered the checkpoint just moments after waking from a luxurious nap. The whole time I could have been at the checkpoint instead of worrying out on the river. I tried not to show my disappointment and stoically asked for a good parking place. My afternoon break had blown my schedule, and we would now be spending the night in Kaltag.

I saw the Montanans as they were leaving and sadly realized our schedules were beyond reconciliation. It had been fun, but my mistakes had cost me too much time. I simply had to resist changing the puppies' rest schedule. I regretted losing the chance to compare my team with young dogs I felt similar to mine, but I needed to keep my priorities straight. It had been enjoyable traveling with them, but I had a job to do.

I left Kaltag at 5:00 the next morning, following Devon Currier through the maze of woods outside the village. The fragrance of the spruce trees made us dance—we were finally off the river! In addition, the run to Old Woman's Cabin was one of the best of the entire Iditarod. My dogs had had grown up training in the woods near the kennel, so they delighted now in racing through the trees.

I had heard about the cabin at Old Woman's since working for Iditarod, and it seemed like a rite of passage to pull into the small clearing in front of the tiny log building. After caring for the dogs, Devon and I built a fire in the woodstove and, like kids in an attic, started going through the leftover food other mushers had left on the table. It was a tradition that you had to leave food here or you would experience bad luck, and from the look of it, every musher facing the two hundred and thirty miles of coast was hedging his or her bets.

Soon Karen and Lesley Monk joined us. After finishing a very difficult race in 1988, Lesley was back on the trail to see what she had missed the first time. I was outside checking on my dogs when Ellie Claus pulled in with her team; Lesley shook her head.

"Puts you to shame, doesn't it?"

Ellie was sixteen years old and traveling the trail alone after her adult companions had bailed out. I had met her my first year working in Rohn when she was twelve and had fallen in love when she knew the exact number of days—2,190—until she would be old enough to run in the Iditarod. I had followed her career and had been delighted on her recent victory in the Junior Yukon Quest. She had joined up with those of us in the back of the pack and was tagging along until Unalakleet. She was learning the trail, still with two more years to go before she could officially do the race.

We made coffee and I felt privileged to be with such fine company. I had regretted losing my other companions, but these folks were fearlessly honest. Here we were away from outsiders, volunteers, and the media. We could confess our mistakes, share both our doubts and tidbits of hard-won wisdom. Food was a big subject. Lesley confessed to living on M&Ms and salmon strips, while Karen brought out a cheesecake bar that was perfect for the Iditarod. I had been chewing on rock-hard energy bars at the high risk of breaking a tooth. Strangely, Karen's treat did not freeze.

"I had a dog that wouldn't eat and I started feeding them to her." Karen's tone was always tongue-in-cheek. "She loved them, but finally I just had to drop her. I didn't have enough cheese bars to get both her and me all the way to Nome."

In the bag of goodies Jeff's daughters had sent me in Galena, there had been one thing I couldn't resist stuffing into my sled, though I had become quite adept freeing my rig of unnecessary burdens. The Magic 8-Ball had been kept hidden; I knew it would have a purpose.

The winds on this side of Unalakleet were famous. In fact, the winds for the next two hundred miles were famous. We rookies feared these coastal storms like we had feared the Gorge. It didn't matter that we had traveled over eight hundred miles; the wind on the coast would humble us, and our first taste would certainly come in the next thirty-five miles. My life on the sea had made me keenly aware of any changes in the air surrounding me, and I now smelled the difference in the wind. I had earlier caught the significance as I chased an errant food bowl that a small breeze skipped across the yard.

Solemnly I now shook the Magic 8-Ball and called for silence. On the bottom side a window revealed answers to yes-and-no questions. "Likely so." "Seems doubtful." "Most definitely, yes!" I had one of these black beauties in my outhouse at home and often consulted it for the day's outlook. Now the crowd of rookies anxiously awaited the answer to my question.

"Will the wind be a problem on the trail to Unalakleet?" We knew the passage down to the coast had plenty of exposed miles that had battered many mushers through the years.

Together we peered down and waited while the liquid settled and the words became clear.

"Decidedly—not!"

Laughter shattered the tense air in the small room, and I carefully set the plastic crystal ball on the table tucked next to the wall.

"Don't ask any more questions!" I said gravely. "That is all we wanted to know." This would be my offering to the old woman of this remote cabin, and I hoped it would appease her.

Devon, Lesley, and I pulled out of Old Woman's Cabin after most of the heat had left the afternoon's sun. Storms could hit this area so quickly that safety only counts after you reach a village, and we wanted to get to the Unalakleet checkpoint as soon as possible.

Where there were no trees, or the trail was notoriously windblown, locals had erected wooden tripods as permanent markers of the trail. Four-foot tall stakes, put in annually by the Trailbreakers, supplemented these. The weather through this area was infamous for being difficult, so every conceivable precaution was taken to keep not only the mushers, but also the locals from getting lost. Silently, I thanked all the strangers for their hard work.

CHAPTER 27

Scent of the Sea

*T*he trail to Unalakleet followed a meandering route through the river valley that bore the same name. If the wind was blowing at home, I would have expected to see whitecaps on the water—but no towering waves. Earlier, I had donned my most protective face mask and now traveled in relative comfort. It was so pleasant that for the second time of the race, I turned on my mini disc player.

David had spent hours putting together one disc of music he thought would be best for me on the trail. Knowing I wouldn't have the patience to change tapes, and trying to find a balance between soothing and riveting—Fleetwood Mac, John Hiatt, Bruce Springsteen, his selection was perfect. With the wind at our backs, the team charged down the frozen Unalakleet River. Like ice skaters, we gracefully glided toward the sun setting on the coast—and once again, I grew teary-eyed. I felt a huge surge of love for David, for these dogs, for this remote village, for the whole country of Alaska.

There are significant moments you are certain will make your top-ten list as you look back on your life—weddings, the births of babies, certain holiday meals—and those last minutes, as I approached the coast, running the Iditarod with a team of dogs I loved and felt an unbreakable bond to, I knew would be hard to ever surpass. The crimson sky, the small yips of excitement from the dogs, the smell of wood smoke and my own complete physical exertion as I kicked the sled to the familiar rhythms of old rock-and-roll tunes—we wait our whole lives for moments like these.

I pulled into the village at 7:10, and I was grateful to see high berms of snow piled into long corridors to hide the resting dogs from the sharpest bite of the wind. Unalakleet was a place of constant wind, and I had once stood in horror watching an Iditarod Air Force pilot take off, straight up, when the winds lifted his plane a hundred yards from where he started the engine.

A local mother and daughter met me at the checkpoint. They had brought a plate of fresh fried fish they had caught through the ice in the river and told me I had been chosen for a school interview. Exhausted, I sat on a cot and dutifully ate every morsel. It was delicious, but I was spent. The Native girl was supposed to be interviewing me, but since she was so shy, I tried to play the role of inquisitor. I was so tired though that I kept getting confused, answering my own questions I posed to myself. And although I appreciated their kindness, I really needed to get to sleep.

After lying down for a few hours, Devon and I left together at 5:30 A.M. It was pitch-black and howling, but we hoped that the coming light of dawn would make the route easier to follow. We lost the trail before we were even out of sight of the checkpoint, and spent a frustrating half hour on a frozen slough looking for trail markers. The wind had swept most signs of a dog trail away; even when we saw a bit of reflective tape in the distance, the path was so slick we could hardly negotiate it. Often my sled slid out of control sideways down the slough, the entire team abreast as we headed north. I wiped out several of the remaining trail-marking lathe myself, and could now understand why there weren't many left for those of us in the back of the pack to navigate by.

We started up a winding trail, and despite the stiff breeze, I immediately began to sweat. I had packed extra food in the sled, heeding the race official's warnings about a huge storm that was going to hit the coast. I knew there was some protection in the Blueberry Hills, so Devon and I were prepared to hunker down there if necessary. I had learned a lesson after feeding my dogs Red Robin hamburgers when I was lost out of Cripple, so I always packed more food than necessary. The sled moved like it had lead in its belly.

Up and around Blueberry Point we kicked, until we suddenly found ourselves skating on an icy creek bed that meandered past an abandoned building. With a rush of emotion, I knew where I was and stopped my team. My dear friend and neighbor Chief had walked here one summer from Shaktoolik to work for the Lomen brothers. The brothers bought reindeer from Native herdsman, and this structure had been one of their processing plants.

Wilmer Asicksick, or Chief, as he was nicknamed during World War II, had been born upriver from where the present-day Shaktoolik rests on a spit of land. When I lived next door to him in Uganik, he was carving replicas of the full-sized sleds his dad had built. From logs of yellow cedar, Chief would spend months honing the honey-colored wood into tiny sculptures of perfection. On a rack near his stove, he slowly steamed the wood into delicate pieces he laced together in the same manner as the real sleds.

Chief was born in 1921 in a village that soon moved. Because the caribou started migrating closer to the next valley, or there were more fish upriver, or less snow in the lee of the mountains, it was not uncommon for villages in Alaska to change locations. In the early thirties Shaktoolik was moved to the coast, closer to the ocean fish and the ships that could venture through the arctic waters for a brief time during the summer months. The ships brought school supplies to the remote location, and when the government built a school, the community stayed.

That is, until a flood in the sixties. Chief's cousin, Laura, was in labor when a huge storm hit that created the waves that covered the spit, which salted the garden plots, which damaged the school. The village moved again, three miles up the coast to higher ground that never flooded, but where the wind blew so hard children learned to walk leaning forward. There is a saying in Shaktoolik: "the wind is our friend." It was a good thing.

When I was a volunteer I had hiked to the abandoned village site with some local boys. Our heavy coats, puffed wide from our bodies, acted as sails in the incessant wind and swept us along the beach. The boys pointed out the broken walls where moss had been used for insulation, and the deep pits where winter ice had been stored to keep the meat cool during the short summers. I found the cement blocks that had formed the foundation of the government school where the children were not allowed to speak their Native language, and where their knuckles had been rapped when they forgot.

I had heard of these things during long hours spent playing Scrabble, and listening to a tiny transistor radio in Chief's smoky cabin. David and I had lived in a tent while we built our house, and Chief's four walls had been my refuge. He would bribe me indoors with fresh venison, and eventually pull out his Scrabble game, threatening to cheat with the tiles of letters. He smoked Pall Malls and hid a list of the best Scrabble words, the ones with q's and z's, in the cellophane wrapper of his cigarettes. He cheated with a flourish of tricky hand moves meant for my eyes alone.

In 1938 Chief had walked the twenty-five miles from Shaktoolik to here, looking for summer employment. As the team patiently paused, I took in the setting. I knew exactly where I was, and for several moments, the worries of the storm were erased as I dwelled on how I had gotten there. Soon enough I would be in Shaktoolik, and after that, in a couple of days, Nome.

We continued on, and then the real climbing began. I could hear the mild-mannered Devon cursing at his sled, the tight turns, and steep climbs of the trail. He was a big man, and his gear was heavy as well. Although speed terrifies me, pure physical exertion tended to fire me up, and seeing Devon's look of disgust, I couldn't resist sharing my enthusiasm.

"There is good reason why so few people have that damned belt buckle, Devon!"

I leaned on my handle bow, taking gulps of the cold air and grinned at him. A coveted, one-of-a-kind belt buckle is given to anyone finishing the Iditarod, and in thirty years, fewer than 1,400 had been awarded. It was an ungainly thing, yet highly cherished by anyone who had earned one.

"We are going to make it!"

Devon had the quiet, good confidence of someone off *The Andy Griffith Show*, and I had liked him the moment we had met. I had known his wife since a coastal blizzard had pinned her down in Shaktoolik during her rookie year, and I felt the same about her. Devon had scratched the year before, but this time he was going to make it; we both knew it. The Blueberry Hills were just not big enough to get this man down, and we continued upward to where I knew my own opportunity to waiver would come. The exit off the thousand-foot hills was a three-mile-long slalom directly down to the long, rocky beach that eventually led to Shaktoolik.

The run was fast, frighteningly fast, and somehow my sled and I tumbled down the chute without tipping over. By the time I got to the bottom, it felt like a completely different day from the one spent slogging through the Blueberry Hills. Above us, the sky was piercingly blue, though we could see a ground blizzard swirling between Shaktoolik and us. I knew the village was just twelve miles away, but I looked wistfully at a shelter cabin tucked tight against the hills.

I had heard countless stories of how these primitive shelters had saved lives, and as a volunteer I had once visited this very cabin, thinking it so small and basic. It was such an unsightly little thing perched here on the edge of the beach, but I was now grateful to see it as we faced the swirling whiteout ahead of us—we had a refuge to come back to if needed.

We started following the trail that paralleled the beach, sticking as close as possible to each other. The wind tore Salem off the trail time and time again, but he was able to keep springing back onto the harder packed snow of the trail. He could feel it with his feet, though I could see nothing myself other than the routinely placed reflective markers. Periodically, Devon and I switched places to give our leaders a mental break. After a few slow miles, the air suddenly cleared.

Ground blizzards are often just a localized band of swirling wind that launches a whirling eddy of old, dry snow. The sky is likely crystal clear just above and beyond the localized storm. Though this may seem comforting, it does nothing to lessen the severity of the dangers. Losing visibility, with blue skies so close at hand, is one of the most frustrating aspects of the storms. The surprise of abruptly breaking free of the whiteout is one of racing's sweetest reliefs.

With the ground blizzard hanging like a curtain behind us, we traveled in sweet, bright sunshine along the beach. It was still windy, but I was excited to spot familiar old Shaktoolik. When I entered the deserted village, I set my snow hook and waited for Devon. I parked my team in front of the house where Chief had grown up, and as I stroked Tahoe's head, I wondered what he would think if he saw me here now.

He wouldn't have cared that I came by dog team; he would have been too excited to show me things. He would have moved like a younger man, and I would have scrambled around after him—crawling up the snowbanks, ducking into the buildings. He would have remembered everything, but wouldn't have spilled it all immediately. He always kept secrets, loved his secrets, but wanted me to dig them out. He would be thrilled that I was finally here to see his country.

I thought of how I had explored the site with the boys my first year as a volunteer, when the wind had blown so steady and cold that I couldn't have imagined any of the buildings ever being warm. I could see an open lee in the frozen sea ice glistening glacier blue in the morning sun. I wondered if the boys would be waiting for me at the checkpoint, if Chief's cousin would be there.

We quickly skimmed over the last few miles and I was surprised to discover that Jeff had flown to Shaktoolik, having finished his race in sixth place. I anxiously watched his face as he looked over the team, but with a thumbs-up he went into the checkpoint and left me alone to my chores. A steady stream of visitors came by as I worked, and between the hugs and introducing my team, I was worn out by the time I had a chance to sit down in the Armory. I did not try to explain much to Jeff, and he did not ask many questions. He soon left to catch the mail plane back to Nome. We'd see him, if all went well, in just a few days.

Shaktoolik had been one of my favorite checkpoints to work in as a volunteer, and the memories made it hard to lie down and rest now. One year Martin Buser pulled into Shaktoolik looking pretty normal for a musher at that point in the race: wind-burned, glassy-eyed, and exhausted. I heard someone quietly ask if he would come speak for a few moments at the school, and saw how wearily he nodded his head yes.

By the time he fed his team, Martin looked so tired I told him I would explain to the children if he wanted to back out—but he refused. I promised at the very least to find him a ride to the school. I understood how important any chance of rest was, but we both knew that the school trip would take precious time off his scheduled break.

We piled into one of the few vehicles in the village and bounced along the snowdrifts to the school. There were 142 kids from kindergarten to twelfth grade, many of the classes sharing the same rooms, the same teachers. The smallest children excitedly greeted him. The older students muttered eager questions. This was someone they had seen on TV; this was a famous person in their school, in their classroom. They could talk to him and he would answer. All they had to do was have the nerve to speak up.

Martin accepted the chair offered and sat down wearily in front of the room, his cooler of dog food at his feet. He quietly talked about life as a dog driver, a kennel operator, a father of two young boys. He told stories of setting goals and accomplishing these goals through patience and hard work. It was just a short talk, but a good one, and I hurried outside to look for our ride back to the checkpoint.

Our ride was gone! Embarrassed, I met Martin as he left the school with the news that we would have to go on foot. It wasn't really a long distance, but after 922 miles, anything would feel tedious. We set off down the road and by odd fortune, a teacher at this moment released her students to come and visit the checkpoint. Twenty, thirty children fell in place around us as we started walking. Many of the kids had posters to hang up at the Armory, and many of these said things such as "Go Martin!" "Buser is #1!" "All the way to Nome, Martin!"

Shifting the heavy weight of the cooler from side to side, he smiled shyly at the children as they skipped and danced around him, trudging steadily toward the checkpoint. A parade! I had to laugh at the sight of this three-time champion leading a procession of children, they with their banners and he wearing tennis shoes in a village famous for its blizzards. This was the magic of the Iditarod!

CHAPTER 28

Possibilities

*W*ith so much talk of the Big Storm coming, I knew we had to get out of Shaktoolik as soon as possible. As a checker, I had often heard the folks in the back of the pack delaying their departures, fearful to cross Norton Sound. It was close to sixty miles across the frozen sea; there was always worry about open water. The ocean currents were still active below the thick pan of ice so that it was constantly shifting, creating rifts and gaping holes. From the trail report, we knew the crossing at this point was relatively stable, but the other big worry was the ground blizzards, which were totally unpredictable. In low visibility, it was possible to wander off the trail and out to open ocean. This created nasty scenarios in a rookie's head.

The Armory was toasty warm, and the company had been particularly fine, but it was time for those in the race to face this next challenge. Nearly everyone geared up to leave close to 6:00 P.M.

I felt sorry for Sandy, who felt the need to rest her dogs another four hours. It would mean she not only would cross the ice in the middle of the night, but that she would be totally alone. She was such a tiny woman, her voice so soft that she seemed more like an urban mom than a dog musher. There was not a single thing about her that someone would describe as tough and yet here she was, the bravest among us all. No one else would have considered crossing Norton Sound alone. Embarrassed, the rest of us prepared our teams to leave in a group.

David Straub and I pulled out together, with Devon, Lesley, and Karen close behind. For years, I had watched the mushers leaving Shaktoolik, fearful for them, having heard about the terrible possibilities in the next leg of the race. Libby Riddles was famous for heading out into a blizzard from here, and though the lead had won her the race in 1985, many others had not been so fortunate. The locals were very careful before they traveled any distance from the village, reading the sky like a weather channel. Clouds over this hill meant one thing: that delicate haze over there meant something else. The wind from the East was good for travel to Koyuk, but bad if you were heading back down the coast to Unalakleet. And always, Mother Nature could just as quickly throw a curveball at you.

After being escorted out of the yard, I followed the trail that dropped into a slough and then wound around a long snow fence before heading out across open country. Each winter, drifting snow created a shear wall twelve feet high against the wooden barrier, diverting a fraction of the wicked northern wind that so often blasted into the village. From the security of the fence, it was fifteen miles across an open marshy peninsula before a peculiar rock marked where the trail launched off across the Sound.

I had only seen Island Rock from small planes. From ground level, it rose so weirdly above anything around it for miles that I was not surprised that the locals had so many ancient stories about it. It certainly made sense to me that a giant had placed it here. I often asked the local children to tell me the legend and was always secretly relieved when they remembered any of the details. Legends could so easily be lost.

As we approached the portal to the sea, day was turning into evening, and my team was turning on. They were rested, happy dogs, and when I put Portland into single lead, I felt the delightful rush of speed. I could see the headlamps of my friends spread out behind me and hoped they were experiencing at least a fraction of the enchantment.

We flew. We flew like you can only fly on a flat trail with stars beginning to show. We flew because one dog leaped forward in complete abandon, with an innate joy of movement. All his teammates had looked around and agreed—and I knew what they felt. We all yearn for the chance to fly under our own power.

I had never placed Portland in single lead, of this I was sure. He was a good ol' boy, but more of a "team" dog than leader material. Though his gait was far from smooth, I loved his bad-boy attitude and the lover's attention I saw when he slowed down long enough to listen to my coos. I had put him in lead out of frustration with his bickering, but laughed with delight as I ran back to the sled. His lunging alone was enough to yank out the snow hook. We were all thrilled.

There are several philosophies about how best to cross long sections of boring sea ice with a team of dogs. By good fortune, my timing had put me exactly where I wanted to be at the perfect time. Early morning and early evening are the two most exciting times to drive a team of huskies. Dogs love to run during the transition from day-to-night and night-to-day as the changing light seems to radically affect their energy level. They smile and wag their tails; they yelp tiny exclamations of delight as they speed along. It was something I had to see play out repeatedly to believe.

With young dogs used to training on interesting trails through changing countryside, I knew the wide expanse of endless white sea would likely bore my puppies into depression. By starting the run in the evening, their natural enthusiasm set a quick pace. As it grew dark, limiting their visual world to what the stars and my headlamp would illuminate, they fell into a methodical trance, and with Portland's enthusiasm, the pace was fast. When I stopped to snack, several immediately barked to continue, and I sang out to join their voices.

As we approached Koyuk, I wondered where in the village the checkpoint was located and worried whether my lead boy knew his commands. I resisted pulling him from his position though. He deserved his glory and proudly led us into the checkpoint like a true professional. We had crossed in just over five hours, honorably close to the speeds of the Montana folks, who had rested nearly twice as long in Shaktoolik.

The checkpoint was well-organized—blue tarps hung from the ceiling of the open room creating cathedral-like niches for the mushers to sleep in. It was a delight to see my good friend Dianne, who had encouraged me through my year of training and bolstered my spirits after the Christmas "bash." I wanted to visit, but felt bone tired. After a hot cheeseburger, I could barely keep my eyes open any longer. I checked on my team, who were parked out of the wind in a straw-filled gully and sleeping soundly, then wearily sank onto the carpet in a far corner.

By five in the morning, I pulled the hook and felt totally disoriented leaving the checkpoint. Paranoia convinced me that I may have ended up on the incoming trail, heading back across Norton Sound. It was still very dark and I simply couldn't see past the extent of my headlamp. Soon I decided to act, and turned the team back around toward the safety and lights of Koyuk.

As the sky began to brighten, I could finally make out tall bluffs off to my left. These landmarks told me that I was indeed following the shoreline of Seward Peninsula and not heading out to open sea. Once again, I had to turn the team around, but I refused to let this send me into a depression. I hadn't lost much time and did not think the dogs were awake enough yet to know what was going on. I took comfort in acting quickly instead of simply worrying, which was more my norm.

The trail was good though the sky was a bit gloomy, and I could see heavier clouds ahead. We passed abandoned buildings—some in total disrepair, while others looked almost inhabitable but drifted over in snow. I thought I recognized Moses Point, an abandoned Federal Aviation Administration post, but it slipped by into the grayness before I could be sure. I really felt like hurrying. My sailor sense told me something was up.

CHAPTER 29

Wind

*E*lim is a village of three hundred people, most of whom live a lifestyle that relies on fishing and hunting for a great deal of their food. Though they often don't have regular jobs, their work revolves around the hunting and fishing seasons when they secure most of the year's food supply. The Iditarod is quite popular with the locals, and as I pulled into the Fire Hall parking lot, children quickly surrounded me. I dutifully went about my chores, half listening to several conversations. Indeed a big storm was building higher up in the hills, and I began to hear what would evolve into a slogan over the next few hours. *Big storm. Big winds. Not wise to go on. Wait.*

Jasper was a checker here and I had heard countless stories during the time we spent together in Rohn. There was no running water at the checkpoint, and the toilet was a five-gallon bucket with plastic bags. To his great chagrin the children of the village flocked to visit and use this improvised bathroom. Jasper complained, telling tales of horror about carrying the delicate bags to the dump, but he couldn't seem to refuse the dark-headed angels. They adored him, and during the rest of the year, back in his home state of Minnesota, he dreamed of ways to make them smile. Jasper Bond was an Iditarod volunteer who lived and breathed the spirit of the event.

The children raced around my team, while my puppies, now quite trail-wise, busily arranged their straw beds preparing for naps. I was the sole musher in Elim until Karen and Kelly Williams, the rookie from Fairbanks, showed up in the early afternoon. The rest of the pack soon followed them, and our teams lined the narrow streets. We clustered around anyone with information about the weather. And then the debates began.

Everyone had an opinion on the weather, and everyone wanted to make sure we understood. "Big storm, very dangerous up on Little McKinley right now. Don't leave. Leave immediately. Wait until morning. Wait until evening. Pack up now—fast! If you don't leave now, you will be here forever. If you leave now, you will die." Everyone had an opinion, and everyone was certain that theirs was right.

We were the back-of-the-pack rookies, and we gathered in anxious huddles to discuss our options. The race judge said go; the locals said stay. Jason Barron called back from White Mountain. He and the other Montanans had made it safely, but the trip had been terrible. He said we all should definitely wait until the weather improved.

The wind was now gusting through the streets, sending pieces of garbage skipping along the snowbanks. The sound of flapping tin made me shiver, and I thought of boats on the open water. Wind was such a part of my life back in Kodiak that I knew I needed to act with great caution. The decision about when to leave Elim would be one of the most important ones of my race.

I looked at my sleeping puppies and added straw to their beds. No doubt they were tired. They were not exhausted, but their young bodies craved a good rest. I knew if I asked them, they would head out into this storm and run hard, never looking back. We had rehearsed for this kind of thing. I had sought out windy spots, and we had practiced. We had trained together for thousands of miles, and they knew I would ask a lot from them, but I would never ask for too much. They would give me absolutely everything they had—of that I was positive.

Up until this point, we had run a fine race. They were having a good time and I was convinced they had no idea of the mistakes I had made. They hadn't known we were lost or that I had cut their rest times to make up for my problems. Bismarck still insisted on playing for a moment before he lay down for a nap, and Tahoe still watched me with adoration while I rubbed her feet, stretching her toes against my fingers.

Salem had led nearly the entire Iditarod, and I knew it would be he who took me over Little McKinley. He had done such a fine job for so many miles, I didn't want to risk ruining this part of the experience for him. He had the makings of a real champion, and with Jeff as his musher, I knew that this puppy's career was just beginning. I had fantasies of him someday replacing his dad, Yuksi, as the top dog at Goose Lake Kennels. I wanted to be sure that next year—when Jeff would likely be racing through these hills with a chance to win—my boy would be bounding enthusiastically down the trail.

As I saw it, my job was to make sure that these dogs knew what it was like to expand their limits, and yet still love to be a sled dog. After running nine hundred miles down the trail, they were pretty content. I could also tell which ones would not likely become the professionals their parents were. Just like people, not every dog is created with equal talents and desires, but recognizing all of this, I was still proud of every single member of this team. I wanted nothing more than to have them happily lope down Front Street when we made it to Nome. So, despite all the advice, or because of some of it, I stayed in Elim nearly twenty-three hours and left when there was light and the wind had lost its edge.

Kelly pulled out in the early evening while Karen and I napped. I was surprised, but at least she had been over the trail before by snow machine and had some idea what to expect. Lesley and G. B. left at three in the morning in a swirling white madness, but I still felt a bit guilty as I lay back down. Karen, Devon, and I had agreed to leave together in the morning, resigned to feeling overly cautious. Devon had scratched the year before and desperately wanted to finish. Karen and I just wanted to stop hearing all the contradictory advice and simply made a decision.

Ken Chase left first, with Devon, Karen, and me close behind, not realizing that we were breaking trail for David, Sandy, and John, who straggled out a while later.

For nearly two hours we followed the frozen coast through deep snow that had the consistency of mashed potatoes. Each time I lifted a foot to help pedal the sled forward, the dense snow clung to my boot, adding pounds to the effort. Even though I had been doing this same workout for nearly a thousand miles, my thighs still ached. I tried to lift my spirits by thinking how shapely they would be by the end of the damned race, but since most of the time I predominantly used my right leg, it was not a pretty image. I'd likely never wear shorts in public again.

At long last, the trail cut up a bank, leaving the heavy coast to begin the climb up the Darby Mountains. I had been unprepared for the Blueberry Hills, but was mentally ready for this climb. I settled into some plain hard work pushing the sled and encouraging the dogs. We passed Ken Chase, but I knew it was because of our youth, not skill, and I did not expect to hold a lead over him for long. The wind had carved meandering canyons into the trail, and I shoved the sled through each miniwall, wondering how much longer my strength would hold out. Up, up, and then briefly, disturbingly, down, the trail wound over the bald hills. We were above the timberline, and the wind was steadily increasing as we climbed. Though the sky looked heavy with snow, occasionally I would see hopeful snippets of blue breaking through the gray.

Near the summit, the wind increased dramatically, and the dogs flattened their ears, crouching as they climbed. I hid behind the handle bow and pushed with all my strength while I sang out encouragement. I couldn't tell if they heard a single word, but I kept singing, as much for me as for them. We crested a knoll, and the wind was so fierce that it shoved Salem to the right, pushing the whole team off the trail's edge. They tumbled downhill, away from the path we'd been following.

"Haw! Haw!" I screamed. No one listened, or no one heard. In a split moment, the land seemed to fall away, and we were weightless, then plunging down the bank in the wrong direction. There was a brief relief, a sweetness to being carried by the wind instead of fighting it—the devil's hand sweeping us faster—but this was quickly replaced with a string of appalling images. I knew the puppies were tired after the hard climb and they would let the wind push them. We were free-falling down the mountain.

The snow had long ago been stolen by the wind, scraped away from this side of the mountain, and we bounced on the frozen hardscrabble ground like a basketball gone awry. I screamed commands to Whoa, and uselessly applied the brake to no avail—rock and dirt having the same frozen consistency. I flipped the sled, and this too was yanked along downhill. Finally, a stanchion caught a frozen tussock and jerked us to a halt. It would not have surprised any of us had we found ourselves on a different planet.

The howling wind burned the skin on my face. I looked back up the hill, stunned silent at all the precious ground we had lost. I was shaking badly and hurt in several new spots, but immediately realized it was no time for self-pity. Potter had already lain down; Lassen was trying to dent the frozen ground with manic pawing. The team could quickly decide they were finished. I fought my way up to Salem and, clawing the frozen grasses, dragged him and the swing dogs back toward the right direction. I gave the dogs a quick pat and let the wind sweep me back to my sled.

A wind that can move a woman can move a dog—even a whole team of dogs—and once again the wind swept everyone downward. Twice more I crawled to the leaders, and both times the winner was the wind, ripping us off the trail and farther down the mountain. The panic in my throat made it hard to breath, and I gasped into my neck gaiter.

Now shaking violently, I again made my way to the front of the team, whispering the name of each dog as I passed. I doubted they could hear me. They were becoming strangers, quickly curling up, tucking their noses deep into their tails. Snow crystals pelted my face, and even my beaver hat couldn't dampen the screams of the gale that surrounded us.

Suddenly I heard a change in the roar of the wind, and looking up saw Ken Chase's team heading straight down the mountain. The roar I heard was Ken, and I could see the angry plume of dirt and snow as he tried to slow the descent. When the team slammed into my sled, they finally stopped. No one looked happy.

Ken stomped over toward his leaders. He did not even try to set his snow hook or flip the sled over—but steamed forward with such command that the dogs shrank away as he passed them. He grabbed his leaders and though he shouted into their faces, I was sure he was speaking to me.

"So you wanted to lead? Now look where you have taken us!"

His team slowly marched back up the hill, and I dragged mine in the same direction. I yelled out commands with a new deepness in my voice that convinced even me—we were climbing this damned mountain and getting to Nome!

There was a delicious moment of sweet relief as we crested the mountaintop, a brief blueness to the sky as I glanced up to give thanks. I quickly looked down on the other side and spotted Golovin Bay. I could see the village on a long spit and it looked so vulnerable surrounded by the white expanse of the sea ice. I knew the pups saw it, too, and we dove forward down the leeward side of the nasty mountains. We were free! There was snow on this side, and the wind on our backs made us feel strong and fast again. I sang out, meaning it, and they knew. We had done it; we had made it past another hurdle.

By midafternoon, we had landed in White Mountain; I was grateful we were required to stay eight hours. We were just seventy-seven miles from Nome, but we needed a good rest after all the hard climbing. And something new dawned on me—I simply did not want it to end. Looking at the faded plywood buildings of this village that I had heard about for so many years, I felt a surge of sadness. My years of work that led me to this place, to do this thing so foreign to anything else in my life, would end soon.

My puppies slept out in their straw beds while I lay on the floor of the checkpoint and numbly wished for just a little more time. I had sent fresh clothes in my drop bag, but they felt stiff and strange against my skin. I couldn't imagine what clean sheets would be like. I suddenly missed being near my dogs, even for such a short time.

I wandered down the hill to the edge of the frozen river where the teams parked, but resisted approaching mine. I could see they were sound asleep, and it was not fair for me to squeeze another emotional crutch from them right now. Though I craved most to put my arms around Tahoe and lie in the straw next to her, I walked back up the hill and eased back into my sleeping bag next to Karen. Her eyes were shut, but I doubted she was able to sleep either.

Our required eight-hour layover ended at 11:45 P.M., and by midnight, the lights of White Mountain disappeared over my shoulder. Thick lazy snowflakes had been falling at the checkpoint, but in mere moments, I went from the cozy arms of civilization into the blind embrace of a winter storm. The wind was not strong, but we were in a whiteout, and my visibility was reduced to having Salem just a faint shadow in lead.

For the next six hours, we traveled from marker to marker. Of course, I could tell when the sled was going up or down, but my concentration was so focused on keeping the beam of my headlamp on the next marker, nothing else existed. The dogs traveled more on their own than they had the entire thousand miles. They strained looking for markers perhaps as much as I did.

This particular area, Topkok, was famous for the blowholes created by canyons channeling winds into demonic forces. I was tired, and the swirling snowflakes dulled my senses. In 1979, when conditions here had gotten too harsh for Joe May and his team, Joe had buried himself in a snow cave to keep alive. I kept reminding myself that I had read of others scratching from the race—this close to Nome—less than seventy miles from the finish line.

The wind had increased as we climbed higher, but visibility was a bigger problem. We followed the blessed pieces of reflective tape one step at a time, and again I silently thanked the volunteer Trailbreakers.

Suddenly the dogs stopped. I could make out a cabin through the swirling whiteness. There was only one possibility, so I felt sure it was the shelter cabin owned by the Nome Kennel Club. That would mean I was thirty miles from White Mountain and had another twenty-five to get to Safety.

A friend of mine had once spent three days with twenty-two other people in this twelve-by-sixteen-foot cabin. Several dog mushers, a few men on snow machines, and some hunters had all found themselves seeking shelter from one of those famous terrible storms. The room was so crowded they had to take turns lying down as the hours turned into days. Luckily, successful caribou hunters were among the lot, and they fed everyone through the ordeal, including the dog teams. Terry had told me about being outside at one point and having something ripped from his hands in the hurricane-force winds. The shake of his head and the dry laugh told more than his words. He was a big man who made his living hunting grizzly bears, and yet the wind had humbled him.

While my dogs snacked, I quickly ducked my head into the cabin just to see how small it really was and for a moment tried to imagine that crowd in this room. It was a basic structure furnished with just a woodstove and a bit of food left from the last inhabitants. Anyone who had ever really needed a shelter cabin was always the most adamant about leaving behind food, and a "fire set," matches ready with a stack of wood to burn. I saw where they were carefully placed, ready to use with frozen fingers if need be—but I was not, so I carefully closed the door behind me.

For a moment, I placed my mittened hand on the back of each dog, bending to call them by name and wipe the snow out of their eyes. Quickly then, I moved back to the sled, and after zeroing in on the next stake, we headed out. Though I could see no trees, I sensed that I was leaving a sheltered cove because the snowflakes immediately increased their devilish dance before my eyes.

Over and over I stopped the sled to sweep the light back and forth in the night, waiting until I caught a bit of orange reflection before moving forward. Several times I had to set the snow hook and then labor up to the front of the team to search from there. The shock of having a marker totally opposite of my dead reckoning made my stomach churn and I laid my hand on Salem's head to regain my calm. I did not want to lose the trail out here. I most definitely did not.

It was totally exhausting, but I had to laugh. Here I was in the last few hours of my Iditarod and still at risk of making a serious mistake that would scratch me out of the race. Or worse. I had been so naïve after coming out of the Dalzell Gorge, thinking the tough part was over. And again in the Burn after the Buffalo Tunnels. And again in Koyuk after crossing Norton Sound. The challenges to this thing were endless. Now I understood why so few had finished, why so many had failed.

Enough mushers had scratched between here and Nome that I knew I needed to stay as alert as possible. Find the stake, swing the leg, and push the sled. Find the stake, swing the leg, and push the sled. It became my new mantra, and it reminded me of my first race as I was coming into Maclaren, but now that event seemed so warm and cozy. We had mentors! We followed a road! This was the real thing. Anywhere locals build shelter cabins just miles from a village, it means that it is easy to die within those short distances.

And then suddenly I sensed we were on pavement and knew I was on the unmaintained road that ran east of Nome to Council. I had driven it one May as a tourist; snows had still blocked travel farther to the ghost town of Solomon. I remembered that I should be passing ancient steam locomotives and other relics of the gold rushers, but I could see nothing. The checkpoint was somewhere ahead of me, and I simply kept pumping.

CHAPTER 30

Final Steps

*N*early six hours after leaving White Mountain, I pulled into Safety, the last stop on the Iditarod Trail. The roadhouse was closed all winter except for these few days in March, and I was tempted to run inside to look, but something stopped me. This was just an ugly old metal building, and somewhere in the darkness several mushers were likely following my tracks. Though I knew it seemed ridiculous, suddenly I felt like I was in a race.

I snacked the dogs quickly, grinning as I thought of films I had seen when DeeDee Jonrowe and Jeff stood in this same place, but were hurrying to win. The checker formally handed over my bib, which I hadn't seen since that long-ago Saturday in Anchorage. I wanted to say something profound about the moment, but simply stood there looking at it. The volunteer hurried away without a word, and I returned to stand protectively near my team. I didn't really want to share these last moments with anyone else.

For several of the final miles on the Iditarod, the trail runs between the road and frozen beach. I had been with Jeff and Donna out here to watch Morten come in last year, and so I was not that surprised to see now the borrowed jeep and arms waving at me. My pups heard the familiar voices, the whistle, and briefly turned their faces—though they never missed a beat. Suddenly I felt the sled shoot forward and everyone was loping. It was as if we were coming home to the kennel after a training run.

I had to steer them around something, and seeing Salem leap—first *Gee* and then *Haw*—to my quiet commands made me cry out, and the first real tears since Takotna burned my cheeks. His ears pricked forward toward town, and he literally bounded down the trail. He looked so damned happy.

Nome has a quirky sense of humor; the architecture, the price of hotel rooms, the annual golf tournament that requires the consumption of alcohol and the donning of parkas. After Christmas each year a temporary forest appears out on the ice in front of town; nearly all the trees within fifty miles, cut and decorated for the holidays, end up repositioned on the frozen sea—in full view until the ocean melts in the spring.

In March, wooden cutouts of gnomes are set up at the edge of town where the Iditarod Trail rises off the beach and enters the city. These colorful figures hold signs of congratulations and promises of hot showers for the mushers, their painted grins enough to make the most trail-worn musher smile. Actually just painted pieces of plywood, the gnomes don't even stand that tall. And yet there at the Gates of Nome, for the first time during all those miles, Salem balked.

My boy had fearlessly crossed the frozen rivers, clawed up the glacier, led the team across the bridge when I was lost. He had been my hero through countless training hours and miles of new trail. He had always been so brave, and yet here he hesitated, scared to pass a plywood cutout of a red-suited gnome. I burst out laughing, and I saw him pause. He knew that laugh. For a moment, he looked back at me, and I swear he grinned. Then, like a true professional, he swung the team wide and onto Front Street.

It was almost ten o'clock on a Sunday morning, and the street was nearly empty. Every single person we passed, though, hesitated on their journey to watch me on mine. Many called out, while others simply stopped and smiled. For the umpteenth time, I was humbled by the kindness of these complete strangers. They genuinely seemed happy for us.

My puppies loped easily down the street toward the burled arch. It was the Alaskan Champs Élysées with the Arc de Triomphe at the end. I could see David off to one side, and I knew the Moms were there, too. For a moment, my mouth went sticky dry; I was almost afraid to travel those last few steps.

Jeff's daughter Ellen jumped on a sled runner as we glided to a stop, and loving arms from the kennel immediately enveloped the team. In the crowd I could see my friend Jeanne had flown up from Kodiak; it had been just five years since we had come here as tourists. Familiar faces beamed at me from behind the snow fence—people I had worked with on the trail, relatives of mushers I had befriended through the years. Martin Buser, the official winner, kindly shook my hand, but quickly stepped out of the limelight. The race marshal gave me a bear hug, and dear Jack Niggemyer, the race manager, pushed through the crowd, his eyes shining. His job offer for me to work on the trail as a volunteer had led to this moment. It had changed my life.

Jeff silently handed me a latte, but I couldn't look him in the eye. The coffee drink was a joke about our common addiction. Many times we had delayed harnessing up or going back out into the cold by boiling water for just one more cup. He had put so much effort into my success, so much time and energy. Would I ever be able to explain how much his allowing me into his world of sled dogs had enriched my life? Standing on Front Street now, I could only whisper.

"Thank you so much."

David shyly approached, and as his arms went around me, I broke down sobbing. There were dark circles under his eyes, and the wrinkles on his face looked thick and permanent, his skin red and blue in the cold air. I could tell the last two weeks had been hard on him, never mind the last years.

"Congratulations, sweetheart," he said and then sighed. "You were gone a long time."

After a long moment, I finally broke away and wiggled my way through the crowd to my team. I worked my way down the line, hugging each one, though I believe they were basking in their own limelight. It had been hard, but they knew that they had done something big, and they preened in the praise and the hands running over their bodies.

When I reached Salem, Donna stepped aside with a knowing smile. I knelt beside him, gently brushing snow crystals off his muzzle. He sunk his head into my arms and held it there, leaning his whole body into mine. I nuzzled the top of his head with my nose and wiped my tears on his velvet ears. When I exhaled a sob, he turned his face up to sink the cool of his nose into my cheek.

For a moment, we were very still, the crowd and city noises disappearing. He seemed so delicate and precious. Had this creature really pulled my sled for over a thousand miles? He nudged me to keep stroking his head and I curled closer to his body. I so cherished our friendship. I was proud that after asking so much from him, he still loved me so completely.

I slowly unwrapped my arms from around his neck, knowing that our journey would, at this moment, end. I took some deep breaths before facing the crowd that surrounded us, and yet I had to smile. I finally understood the hesitation I had seen on other mushers' faces here beneath this arch, a thousand—a million—miles from somewhere else.

Last Run

*I*n late March I took one last run with my pups. Jeff and I went out to the Denali Highway, and at one point he asked if he could drive my team. After charging up a few long hills, he gave them back to me with a nod and brief pat on the back. "They look wonderful," he said quietly before walking back to his own team. "You did great." I was glad he couldn't see my face during the next few miles, but I knew he understood how hard it would be for me to say good-bye to them.

Upon returning to Uganik, I hauled the heavy boxes from the floatplane up to our house and started unpacking the details of my northern life: the fleece pants, the mittens, my headlamp, my big boots. Everything about the race was quickly taking on a dreamlike quality. The fur hat seemed familiar, but it had been new before the race—had I really worn it into this beaten shape? Had I really worn it for fourteen days across Alaska by dogsled?

I looked out across the ocean, but the musky smell of dog turned me back toward my boxes. I knew if I stopped and let myself imagine the feel of Tahoe nuzzling my cheek, or wonder for a moment where Salem was, I would cry, but the boxes stacked around me were waiting, as was David, who wanted a boat ride to celebrate my return.

Instead I quickly made myself think of Lassen the first time she was in lead all by herself—and her expression when she caught the headless hare that had fallen from the sky—that leap of pure innocent joy—and just like always, she made me laugh.

Tazi wagged her tail as I jumped into the boat, and David pointed to a raven flying overhead, chasing one of my beloved bald eagles, just having fun. And we were off.

POSTSCRIPT

*T*ahoe, Houston, and most of the other dogs in my team have now made several trips to Nome—some faster than others. I have followed their careers with the passion of a proud parent. In 2004 David and I did the Serum Run, a reenactment of the 1925 relay that saved the children of Nome from diphtheria. My sled was pulled by Lassen's pups—the precious metal litter: Zinc, Pewter, and Tin.

Yuksi is now the gray-muzzled grandpa. He is still the grandsire, but is wintering with us, pulling me on my skis with the same passion he always had for racing.

Salem, the prince, knows his place at the kennel though. He has the doghouse up front and on campouts he sleeps with the boss. I smile to see so many of his traits in the youngest litters—the joy of going down a new trail, the huge desire to please.

David and I built a cabin in Denali and now commute between two of the most beautiful places in the world. Last year I traded a load of fish for one sled dog—but just one, I promised.

▲ **Salem, Jeff King, and Bronte.** Salem was awarded the coveted Golden Harness Award for his outstanding performance in Jeff's winning team. (I have never been prouder of anyone in my whole life.) PEGGY FAGERSTROM PHOTO

About the Author

*L*isa Frederic has been blessed in living the Alaskan dream. After coming north for summer employment, she spent the next two decades fishing for wild salmon off the coast of Kodiak Island. She and her husband built a home in an isolated bay, eight hours by boat from the closest town. They make their own electricity and get mail once a week by seaplane. There are more bears than people in their neighborhood.

A vacation in 1997 turned Lisa's life upside down when she visited Nome to see the end of the Iditarod Sled Dog Race. Five years later she was shocked to find herself committed to driving a dog team across the state. In 2002 she completed the 1,049-mile Iditarod Trail Sled Dog Race as a rookie at forty-two years old.

These days she writes and gives tours inside Denali National Park, trains sled dogs for Jeff King, and commutes to the ocean waters around Kodiak to fish commercially. Lisa is making plans for her next midlife adventure.

"There is no greater faith

than the faith of a great dog."

— Anonymous